GARDENING
FOR OUR
CHANGING CLIMATES

Published by Angela Patchell Books Ltd
www.angelapatchellbooks.com

registered address
36 Victoria Road, Dartmouth
Devon, TQ6 9SB

contact sales and editorial
sales@angelapatchellbooks.com or
angie@angelapatchellbooks.com

ISBN: 978-1-906245-03-0

book design by Toby Matthews
book concept by APB
photographs from botanikfoto

printed by SNP Corporation

GARDENING
FOR OUR
CHANGING CLIMATES

A GREENER
LIFESTYLE

GILL FARRER-HALLS

CONTENTS

Gardening for Changing Climates

As the title of this book clearly indicates, the climate worldwide is changing. These changes in our weather patterns will impact on all areas of lifestyle, but perhaps one of the most obvious areas to consider is gardening.

"By accepting the climactic changes positively and working with them creatively, gardening can still be fun and enjoyable."

Already we have seen in the last few years an increased frequency of hot, dry summers. These are interspersed with sudden, violent rainstorms that often cause local flash flooding. When these conditions are followed by mild, dry winters, the result is a dramatic fall in water tables and seriously depleted reservoirs.

These new climactic conditions pose a real challenge, and this means first and foremost that conserving water in our gardens is progressively more important. We need to rely less on drawing from the mains water supplies, which are increasingly subjected to extended periods of restricted use during the summer months. Summer droughts are here to stay, and we need to consider how to adapt our gardening methods to accommodate the changing climate.

A comprehensive drought resistant strategy in the garden must be based on holistic principles to have maximum effect. Coping with reduced rainfall and water restrictions doesn't just mean we should simply water our plants less frequently. We need to consider a combination of water-conserving measures, as well as carefully choosing plants for their tolerance of drier conditions.

In Chapter One we take a look at the different ways of adapting to climate change holistically. For instance, this includes investigating thoroughly water conservation, not just thinking that by saving rain water in water butts we have solved the problem. We also need to find strategies to minimize moisture loss in the soil, such as improving the soil structure by digging in compost, and applying a layer of mulch on the surface.

The importance of making your garden attractive to wildlife is described in Chapter Two. The drought resistant garden is the subject of Chapter Three. Here we consider both the problems and the opportunities posed by dry conditions generally, and look at a real life large garden project.

In the tropical exotic garden chapter fantasies of a tropical paradise can be seen to become possible in your own garden to some extent, and we see how a small exotic, tropical garden might look. Let your imagination and creative inspiration roam freely amongst the suggested tropical plants that can now thrive in our changing climate.

The currently fashionable Mediterranean style of gardening is described in Chapter Five. It is salutary to consider that the Mediterranean weather conditions are increasingly with us already as our climate changes. Here we consider a container garden project, so even those with just a sunny windowsill, tiny roof terrace or small patio can find ideas to create a miniature Mediterranean garden.

The book ends with an alphabetical listing of plants suitable for the various gardens described. Comprehensive references and color pictures help you decide on which plants you might like to include in your garden, and information on planting and care is included.

Overall, the book offers encouragement to embrace our changing climate, and advice on how to adapt gardening methods to accommodate the new conditions. By accepting the climactic changes positively and working with them creatively, gardening can still be fun and enjoyable.

Lilies and Japanese Forest Grass complement each other in a mixed border

CHAPTER 1

GOING GREEN IN THE GARDEN

Plants have thrived in their natural state for many centuries in woods, grass lands and forests without any human intervention. Although contemporary organic gardening methods cannot claim to exactly recreate such a paradise or Garden of Eden, nonetheless organic gardening follows Nature's paradigm as much as possible. The word 'organic' simply means 'of living origin'. However, when the word organic is used to describe gardening it has a broader remit that includes the whole process of growing plants as naturally as possible.

Adapting to Climate Change Ethically

"One of the most evocative images of childhood is a meadow full of wild flowers. Unfortunately it's one that few of our children are ever likely to enjoy: intensive agriculture, combined with massive use of herbicides, has all but done away with the meadow. But gardeners can make a difference by having their own wildflower meadows, and now is a good time to plan one."

(CAROL KLEIN)

We are today living in a world where global warming is a current reality, rather than a future potential. Despite being dismissed by some short sighted people as a doom prophecy, scientific assessments of annual mean temperatures and rainfall levels demonstrate unequivocally that the world's climate is changing rapidly – and that the cause is at least partly down to human behaviour, such as increasing levels of carbon dioxide emissions.

Weather patterns around the globe can be seen to be shifting into less predictable patterns that tend to the extreme, so hurricanes, floods and droughts will become more frequent. It is clear that we need to adapt our way of living to accommodate these climactic changes, and because human behaviour is at least partly responsible for global warming and climate change, then the most appropriate response is to adapt our lifestyle sympathetically and ethically. Politically, the process is only just beginning, but as individuals we can still make an important difference – and start making it now.

The Ginger Garden in the Botanic Gardens, Singapore is a good example of a tropical exotic garden

A CHANGE IN LIFESTYLE

There are many areas of lifestyle that we can change; for instance we need to improve conservation of energy and other natural resources. In the home we can use energy efficient light bulbs, turn the heating down a few degrees and improve wall, boiler and loft insulation. This book focuses particularly on what can we do in the garden to adapt to climate change ethically. However, it also suggests that we can still enjoy growing flowers and plants without feeling guilty that we are wasting precious, natural resources such as water.

One of the major practical implications of global warming is that there will be less water overall. Rainfall is predicted to increasingly fall in short, violent, infrequent bursts. This means there will be long periods without rain, the soil will dry out and then when the heavy rainfall does finally occur, instead of sinking down and reinvigorating the soil, much of the water will run off, taking with it the precious topsoil.

One answer to this problem is simply to water the plants more frequently, but this is a wasteful, uncaring option that does not address the long-term implications of climate change. It is also impractical when we recall that in several recent summers there have been water shortages and hose pipe bans.

Pride of Madeira, Viper's Bugloss, and Erysimum bicolor mix together in a colorful display

Climate Change in the Garden

One important ethical and environmentally friendly way to accommodate climate change in the garden is to grow drought resistant plants. These can be gradually introduced into the garden to replace the moisture loving plants that used to be suitable for, and indeed flourished in, our gardens before global warming arrived.

Going Green Tip

If you can't change the conditions – the increasingly long, hot, dry spells with sudden violent winds and storms characteristic of global warming – then you must adapt how you garden to cope with them.

The traditional cottage garden will eventually mostly become a relic of the past, to be replaced by exotic, tropical and Mediterranean gardens. This is a future scenario – not just a potential vision, and one that will arrive perhaps sooner than we think.

Although it will be sad to lose some of the cottage garden favourites beloved of our temperate climate, it can be a joy to welcome other plants to the new warmer conditions that

Incorporating trellis and climbing plants into your garden creates a natural windbreak

in previous years would not have survived the cold winters and heavy frosts. There will always be specialised gardens, and gardeners can always keep a few favourite traditional temperate plants. But the innovative gardener will welcome the opportunity to introduce other, different plants into their gardens, along with new gardening methods that represent an ethical, environmentally friendly adaptation to climate change.

It should be remembered that every country has different regions with some variation in climate. For instance in the UK there are the cold northern areas, the wet, cool Lakeland District and the warmer temperate southwest. Then there is the relatively arid region of East Anglia, where the famous dry gardens of Beth Chatto are located. She incorporates plants into her gardens that need virtually no watering and little attention. These plants have naturally adapted to survive in dry conditions, and yet still provide a stunning display of foliage and flowers. The gardeners of East Anglia have generally survived the recent hot, dry summers and consequential hose pipe bans with relative ease, compared to the rest of the UK.

HOW TO COPE WITH ADVERSE CONDITIONS

At this point the questions arise – how do you manage a successful garden in such difficult conditions? How will gardeners cope with adapting to climate change ethically? The main point to bear in mind is adaptation. If you can't change the conditions – the increasingly long, hot, dry spells with sudden violent winds and storms characteristic of global warming – then you must adapt how you garden to cope with them.

For instance, wind can be a real nuisance in the garden, blowing over our precious delphiniums and other tall flowering plants. Wind is also very drying, blowing in gusts over the surface of the soil and taking with it the moisture.

NATURAL WINDBREAKS

Designing and laying out your garden with natural windbreaks can lessen wind damage, which is likely to increase as winds become stronger. You can plant hedges, and grow trees that do not require lots of water, and – with the help of a little trellis and climbing plants – create 'rooms' or semi separate areas of the garden. These individual garden spaces slow down considerably the wind and prevent both plant damage and moisture loss.

There are several vital areas of going green in the garden to consider which will be explored in the rest of this chapter. Adopting organic methods and working with the principle of holism by understanding that all things are interrelated is a fundamental first step.

Digging potatoes: growing your own organic vegetables is part of the Green Movement

Going Organic

A quick look back over the last fifty years or so reveals clearly that an increasing number of people have developed the desire for a more natural lifestyle. They have also understood the importance of ethical responsibility and the need for a considerate attitude towards the environment. These two concerns are united in the philosophy of organics. A major part of the Green Movement, organic gardening is today seen as a positive counter force to the excessive use of chemicals in all aspects of our lives.

"Every garden can be run organically, from the smallest to the largest, whatever the location. Even in the middle of a city you can create your own miniature ecosystem"

(PAULINE PEARS & SUE STICKLAND)

On hearing the word organic, most people usually think first of organic vegetables, fruits and other crops, and then of how these were originally grown and produced. The traditional, natural method of local subsistence farming was practised successfully until population growth and urbanisation created a demand for large quantities of food to feed the populations of huge cities.

Responding to this need, intensive farming methods were soon developed, and alongside the introduction of battery chickens and massive farms came the use of agro-chemicals. Unfortunately the use in intensive farming of agro-chemicals such as herbicides, pesticides and chemical fertilisers can cause long term damage to the countryside and the birds, insects and animals that inhabit it.

It is a similar story, but obviously to a lesser extent, in our own gardens. If we use chemical fertilizers to grow our flowers, pesticides to deter insects and other garden pests, and weed killers to keep the paths and patios clear, then our gardens are contributing to the overall destruction of our natural habitat. Increasing numbers of people are also developing allergies to these chemicals, as well as other illnesses associated with them.

HOW TO GO ORGANIC

Organic gardening therefore means growing plants naturally, without pesticides and chemical fertilizers. In this way we ensure that the surrounding environment is sustained healthily, and neither wildlife nor the countryside is exploited. It is now generally accepted that organic gardening methods can and do work, and that you can have a beautiful garden without compromising either the environment or your own health.

However, deciding to become an organic gardener means somewhat more than changing your brand of fertilizer, or stopping spraying your roses. The organic philosophy involves a change of attitude, from a short-sighted linear view that suppresses symptoms, to a holistic long-term vision that understands and responds to cause and effect. An organic garden is a natural garden that encourages Nature in all her bio-diversity.

Fernleaf Yarrow and Mexican Giant Hyssop both have pretty flowers that attract wildlife

Going Green Tip

Try to create and tolerate a messy garden; obsessive neatness in the garden encourages a sterile environment. Leaving dead leaves, grass cuttings and so forth to rot down into the soil, reduces the need for extra plant food.

Let's consider weeds. An unthinking chemical solution is to see a weed, regard it as undesirable and zap it with a powerful weed killer. The organic gardener in the first place may not regard the plant as a weed at all. Although we can technically label a plant 'a weed', if it has pretty flowers and encourages wildlife then perhaps it can be viewed as a self-seeding asset. Even if it is regarded as undesirable – maybe a weed that has few benefits, spreads uncontrollably and chokes your other flowers – then spending the time and effort to dig out the roots properly is a better solution than a spray.

The organic garden is a holistic environment that is much more than the sum of its parts. All living things in the garden form an ecosystem and are interrelated and interdependent. Let's return for an example to the pretty flowering 'weed' in the previous paragraph that has been allowed to thrive rather than been chemically executed. A closer look reveals that it is covered with ladybirds, which then fly off to the next plant and start eating the greenfly off it, thereby naturally protecting the plant.

WHAT DOES AN ORGANIC GARDEN LOOK LIKE?

An organic garden has a broad mixture of plants, because garden pests and diseases are then less likely to spread widely and are easier to control. Diversity is part of Nature's pattern. It's important to include many flowers – including the odd flowering 'weed' – as these encourage wildlife attracted by the nectar and pollen. These garden friends are useful for the overall health of the ecosystem.

Try to create and tolerate a messy garden; obsessive neatness in the garden encourages a sterile environment. Leaving dead leaves, grass cuttings and so forth to rot down into the soil, reduces the need for extra plant food. A haphazard woodpile encourages a range of wildlife such as hedgehogs, ground beetles and centipedes, which will eat slugs, caterpillars and aphids. Unless you know definitely otherwise, do not assume visiting creatures are pests; even if they are not an actual garden friend they may well be harmless.

In Nature's wild gardens everything is part of a natural cycle, with nothing new brought in and nothing taken away. Although we cannot be quite as pure as Nature, recycling whenever possible is an important organic consideration. For instance, use dead leaves to create leaf mould, and include dead weeds and grass cuttings in your compost. The resulting natural fertilizers can be used as plant food.

Because the organic garden is a natural garden, wild flowers – and the odd weed! – form an integral part of it. Problems with garden pests tend to arise when too many 'unnatural' plants are introduced. By unnatural we mean highly cultivated plants, such as specially grown hybrids and so forth. This does not mean your prize dahlias and roses must go, merely that they should be interspersed with wild flowers, self seeders and other plants that naturally acclimatise in your garden.

Making your garden completely organic is not easy, but adhering to basic organic principles as much as possible is simple. The main points are to refrain whenever possible from using chemicals, encourage wildlife and diversity of plants, and recycle your garden waste. More useful tips for sustainable, organic gardening can be found over the next few pages.

Spider Flower and Chinese Fountain Grass provide contrasting textures

This informal perennial garden provides a haven for wildlife

Mexican Daisy and watering can: using a watering can instead of a sprinkler helps save water

Water Consciousness

"I really don't hold with watering. Of course I water new plants in and I do give extra water to keep them going until they are established. But I do not make a practice of watering the garden in periods of drought"

(BETH CHATTO)

Droughts will inevitably become more frequent as our climate changes due to global warming, and so it is prudent to learn as many diverse ways as possible to conserve water and use it minimally. Below are described several tried and trusted techniques of water conservation. However – as the quotation from Beth Chatto indicates – learning how to reduce the plants' need for water in the first instance is a necessary part of adapting to climate change holistically, so also included are tips on how to reduce the need for watering plants in the garden.

Going Green Tip

Make sure the butt you choose comes with a rain-pipe diverter kit. This is an easily fitted device that cuts into your drainpipe and diverts the water into the butt.

ne simple tip is to plant out new plants in autumn rather than in spring, as less watering is required for new plants to establish themselves at this time of year. Although this requires advance planning – and avoiding spontaneous purchases at the garden centre in spring – autumn plantings grow successfully early in the year and are well established before the arrival of hot, dry summer weather.

WATER BUTTS

An obvious place to start water conservation is to purchase a water butt. Installing a water butt, or an old fashioned wooden barrel with a cover, or – for larger gardens – a water tank is an easy way to save and store rainwater. Make sure the butt you choose comes with a rain-pipe diverter kit. This is an easily fitted device that cuts into your drainpipe and diverts the water into the butt.

The water butt needs to have an accessible tap near the base. It's a good idea to place the butt on a stand – thereby raising the base of the butt – so repeated filling of your watering can from the tap does not give you a bad back from leaning over too much. You should also purchase one of the many commercially available biological treatments, composed of natural plant extracts, which keep the stored water fresh.

IMPROVING THE SOIL

Poor quality soil allows water to drain through quickly, or to run off the surface, so improving the soil is also important.

The best way to give your soil better structure – and add nutrients – is to dig in well-rotted organic matter, which will improve the soil's moisture retention capacity.

You can also apply a surface mulch of the same compost or manure, or you can mulch using bark chippings or leaf mould. All these materials will naturally break down and be incorporated into the soil, improving the structure and adding nutrients. Mulching also helps keep the soil free from weeds, which both lessens work and retains the moisture for the plants you value.

WATERING

When watering is absolutely essential, then irrigate only in the evening when it is cool; this can prevent moisture loss due to evaporation. This is particularly true of daytime watering during warm, sunny conditions, which can also damage fragile foliage if the sun's rays are allowed to "burn" off drops of water.

Avoid frequent and light watering as these techniques encourage shallow rooting and exacerbate moisture loss. Watering is best done thoroughly and infrequently; for instance during periods of extended summer drought water only once a week, but ensure you really soak the ground thoroughly so the water sinks down to the roots. Another water saving technique is to water around the base of your plants, not over them, as this also reduces evaporation loss.

The Bromeliad House in the National Orchid Garden, Singapore is under cover providing a suitably moist, warm environment

Green Fingers Tip

Mix the water saving granules with plant food granules, to reduce the need to feed your plants.

LAWNS

With increasingly frequent droughts becoming a normal part of weather patterns it's now time to consider reducing the size of – or even eliminating – your lawn. Although most lawn grasses will usually survive a period of drought without watering, your lawn will look dreadful – brown and dry as if it were dead. In fact long periods of drought weaken turf considerably, allowing moss and weeds to establish. Ideas on aesthetically pleasing substitutes for lawns are given in more detail later.

DROUGHT-BUSTER PRODUCTS

There is quite a variety of water conserving products for the garden available these days now that more and more people are conscious of the need to use water carefully. For instance, there are some simple syphoning sets that allow you to recycle the grey water from your bath that would otherwise be wasted down the drain. These systems work by simply placing one end of a flexible PVC hose in the bath, and dropping the other end out of the window into your garden. You then connect the hose to your garden hose with a standard connector, squeeze the pump to get the draining process started and then gravity keeps the water flowing.

Incorporating water saving granules – such as the proprietary brands Raingel and Aquagel – into compost or soil reduces the need to water plants to only once a week or ten days. The granules are composed mostly of a non-toxic potassium-based polymer, which on average hold about 100 times their own weight in water. One application lasts for the entire growing season and helps prevent soil and compost from drying out.

A handy tip is to mix the water saving granules with plant food granules, which simultaneously reduces the need to feed your plants. Most commercial brands of water saving granules are designed for multiple uses, such as in window boxes, patio plant containers, hanging baskets and even flowerbeds.

IRRIGATION SYSTEMS

There are many different irrigation systems available. Although their primary purpose is often just to provide an automatic watering facility, they also function to reduce water use. A simple irrigation system consists of a porous, recycled rubber pipe laid along the flowerbed that allows water to seep out near your plant roots. Such pipes can be used above ground or buried a few inches underneath the soil. More complicated irrigation systems have timers, and branches off the main pipe that are fixed into different plant pots or baskets.

Stone paving and shrubs combine to reduce lawn size in this classic Mediterranean garden

> *"Making compost enriches our lives almost as much as it does our gardens. It seems to harmonize our being here with the way the world ought to be."*
>
> (Stu Campbell)

Composting

Improving the soil in your garden by forking in compost increases the humus content and is of great importance. Not only does this mean that you need to use less or no fertilizer, but improving the soil structure also increases its ability to retain water. Less water loss means less watering, so less waste of this precious resource.

Making basic compost is fairly simple, though composting can also be quite complex if you choose to explore the subject in depth. So it's a great idea to think now about starting to transform your kitchen and garden waste into compost. After a while you will have the satisfaction of digging your home-made compost in to your flowerbeds to improve your soil structure and feed your plants.

There are a variety of nutrients in compost that help plants thrive, particularly potassium, nitrogen and phosphorous as well as many other minor micro-nutrients. Composting is a completely natural process of decomposition and decay that happens naturally whenever plants shed leaves and die down. Any forest floor for instance is covered with dark, crumbly leaf mould that is Nature's compost. This is Nature's way of recycling waste into a valuable commodity that helps new plants to thrive.

Composting can be described as giving something back to the land to balance out what is taken from it in a completely natural way. A compost heap or bin is therefore an integral part of any organic garden. Composting also reduces household waste that would otherwise be put into land-fill sites, so it provides an ethical alternative to contributing to the poisoning and destruction of our environment.

What Items Can You Compost?

The wider the variety of ingredients you put in to your compost, the wider variety of nutrients it will produce, so include in your compost as many of the following as possible.

From the kitchen and house: vegetable and fruit peelings have a high content of nitrogen and carbon. Tea-leaves, coffee grounds, crushed eggshells and leftover grain or vegetable based foods are good, but avoid meat or fish as this attracts rats. Hair, paper and shredded cardboard in small amounts add dry bulk and create air spaces, which helps prevent the compost going off and turning into a slimy mess. However, avoid newspaper or glossy magazines as the inks contain tiny quantities of undesirable chemicals. The contents of the vacuum cleaner compost well as long as you do not have synthetic carpets.

From the garden: most weeds are fine as seeds are destroyed by the heat generated by the decomposition process, but avoid roots of insidious creeping weeds such as nettles, bind weed and couch grass as these will thrive in your compost heap. Grass cuttings, finely chopped prunings from deciduous plants and dead flowers are all good. Avoid evergreen prunings and leaves as these take a long time to decompose, although tiny amounts finely shredded add valuable nutrients. Some people create separate leaf mould heaps as the eventual resulting compost is nutritious for flowering plants.

How to Make Compost

STEP 1: Decide on a suitable site for your compost heap or bin. Make sure it is positioned near enough to the house for easy access, but not so close that it is unsightly or might become smelly.

STEP 2: Clear the space of all objects, weeds etc, and then either install a compost bin or mark out a square of about four or five feet wide and long for a compost heap.

STEP 3: Start adding your kitchen, house and garden waste as described. Finely chop or shred any large objects, and at the beginning include some chopped straw if possible to add some bulk.

STEP 4: As the layers begin to build up, include some scrunched up paper and cardboard every few inches so the compost is aerated and does not become too soggy.

STEP 5: Once a month or six weeks turn and mix the compost with a pitchfork or similar. Check the compost is moist, but not too wet, and add water or chopped dry straw to remedy if necessary.

STEP 6: After several months begin checking the base of the heap or bin from time to time to see if the compost is ready to use. Ready compost is a crumbly non-smelling brown mixture that is easily recognised.

Flowers and vegetables intermingled freely in this allotment garden

Compost Bin or Compost Heap?

A compost heap is the easiest way to start composting. If you have a large garden, or a medium sized garden with a screened off area, then a compost heap is ideal. Site the heap at far end of the garden where it will not be an eyesore, nor will the smell permeate near the house or patio. If there is enough space, a good idea is to have two heaps, as this will give you compost at different stages of decomposition.

Other than aesthetic considerations, there are few disadvantages to a compost heap, although the main complaint is that it can take up to a year to obtain ready compost. However, you need to build your compost heap with care and attention. A common fault is to not have a wide enough base, so the heap becomes top heavy and topples over. To avoid this, when you start your heap cover a patch of ground about four or five feet wide and long and build up from there.

Try to create sandwich like layers alternating wet and green materials with dry, withered matter. Light rainfall will keep the compost heap sufficiently wet, whilst covering the heap with a tarpaulin during heavy rain prevents it becoming waterlogged. Turning or forking the heap every couple of weeks helps aerate the compost.

A compost bin is ideal for small gardens, neater than a heap and can be sited near the house. A bin holds heat better than a heap, thus speeding up decomposition, and the lid keeps off rain. In hot dry weather you might need to water your compost to prevent it drying out. It can be awkward to turn compost in a bin, but you can help aeration by adding scrunched up paper from time to time.

Speeding up the Compost

Making compost in your garden at home is similar to Nature's rotting, though you may want to speed up the process a little. To quicken the composting process you can apply a compost activator. There are many commercially available proprietary brands of compost activator, but you can easily make your own.

A mixture of young nettles and comfrey leaves mixed into the compost with a pitchfork helps activate the compost. Pond weed is good if you have a pond. Additionally, urine contains a good balance of enzymes to heat the compost thereby speeding up the process. Adding small quantities of urine along with nettles and comfrey creates an effective home-made compost activator.

The compost is ready when you notice a brown crumbly substance at the bottom of the heap or bin. Carefully remove the compost from the heap; compost bins have a flap at the bottom for easy removal of ready compost. Dig this in to your borders, or use as a mulch, applying a layer on bare soil around your plants.

Compost bin by CleanAirGardening.com

A mixed perennial border in full bloom, mid-summer

Begonias and Marigolds surround an eco-friendly solar light

Mulching

Mulching is somewhat similar to composting, and a discussion on mulching follows on logically from a look at composting. Alongside digging in compost once every few years, applying a good layer of mulch on the surface of your flowerbeds and borders is one of the most effective ways to retain moisture in your garden soil. Another excellent reason to mulch is that applying a thick layer will help to prevent weeds springing up between your plants.

Aim for a layer of organic mulch that is a minimum of two to three inches thick and up to six inches thick; this will lessen moisture loss from the surface of the soil and keep the moisture near the roots of your plants where it is most needed. Make sure you apply the layer of mulch when the soil is thoroughly soaked through from rain to maximize moisture retention.

Mulching the surface of your soil is far less work than digging in compost, which is a major advantage for anyone with a bad back or who is short of time. Forking over your beds thoroughly once a year used to be considered a gardening requisite, but many gardeners now consider this practice counterproductive.

Although digging has the advantage of aerating the soil – making life easier for worms and newly installed plant roots – digging too frequently destroys the soil structure. Digging also disrupts the microscopic bio-diversity of organisms in the soil so only dig when absolutely necessary.

There are quite a few different materials you can use as mulch, but they basically fall into two main categories:

"In the last three of four years, my garden has been vastly improved in looks, performance and maintenance by mulches. I find that the rate of growth of plants under a mulch is quite astonishing."

(BETH CHATTO)

organic mulches and inert mulches. Organic mulches such as compost, manure and bark chips have the added advantage of breaking down and adding nutrients, such as the essential nitrogen, to enrich the soil. However, these need to be topped up more frequently than inert mulches, which are more or less permanent. Hard working earthworms will over time drag organic mulch down into the soil where it will be available to feed your plant roots.

ORGANIC MULCHES

If you have a compost heap or bin, then your own home-made compost is the cheapest and most readily available mulch. However, you need an awful lot of compost to make a good, thick layer of mulch, so your own supplies may well need to be supplemented with other organic matter. If you have only a limited supply of compost, then apply a thin layer directly onto the soil and top up with a layer of one of the other organic mulches.

Well-rotted manure is good if your soil is very poor and lacking in humus. Avoid fresh manure, as this is too potent and can "burn" the roots of plants and kill them. Grass clippings are convenient if you have a lawn, and make quick, moist mulch, though it may need topping up quite often. Leaf mould, composted bark and wood chips, straw and hay, shredded tree and bush clippings all make good organic mulches. Spent hops – if you live near a brewery – are also fine.

Lavender, roses and mallow interplanted with annuals make a colorful display

Although peat makes excellent, long lasting and sterile mulch, it should no longer be used, despite the fact that some garden centers still supply it. Too many precious peat bogs have been dug out and destroyed already, and there are plenty of other more ethical alternative organic mulches.

Straw and hay are useful to make a coarse, thick layer that is especially good at the back of wide borders spread between trees and larger shrubs. Bracken can be mixed in if available. Once rainfall has flattened the straw and made it sodden and heavy it becomes fairly impervious to being blown away by wind, and often lasts for a full growing season, or even longer.

For the front of the border and amongst the smaller, more delicate herbaceous plants and annuals you need finer and more aesthetic mulch. Composted bark chips are good here although make sure you obtain a fine grade. Too coarse bark chips have a tendency to slip off each other and allow the more determined weeds to grow through quite easily. However, with very fine bark chips you may need to neaten the layer of mulch after strong winds have blown them about. A mulch of bark chips will probably need topping up a little bit each year.

INERT MULCHES

There are both practical and aesthetic considerations for using inert mulches. Some plants, especially alpines, object to being surrounded by damp, organic mulch and have a tendency to rot in winter. These plants flourish best with a layer of gravel, about two inches deep, whereby rain drains through quickly, weeds are suppressed and moisture loss is much reduced.

Strawberries on a layer of straw mulch are protected by a net

There are many inert types of mulch to choose from including gravel, spar, limestone and granite chips, flint, pebbles and rocks. Such a variety of size, shape and color offer the potential to create intricate and elaborate designs. You need to be quite certain about your choice of inert mulch before applying it because – unless disturbed – it will last for many years. Apply inert mulches to moist soil and create layers between two and three inches thick.

Inert mulches are particularly suitable for low water and drought resistant gardens, and you can borrow many ideas from traditional Mediterranean style gardens. For an exotic, desert look, try interspersing yuccas and agaves planted in a spacious but defined pattern with a thick coarse gravel or pebble mulch in between. This quick and simple planting idea can create a quite dramatic almost instant effect.

You can unleash your artistic side and create beautiful patterns with the different textures, shapes, sizes and colors of stones available. For instance, you can use the pale shades of limestone and marble chips together with red granite chips in a simple but effective two-tone pattern to fill the spaces between low growing plants such as sempervivums and alpines.

Alternatives to Grass Lawns

Drought resistant, Mediterranean and tropical gardens are all overwhelmingly characterized by an absence of formal lawns because they do not thrive outside a temperate climate.

A wildflower meadow makes an attractive alternative to a lawn

Green Fingers Tip

Leave your lawn mowings in place as mulch, thereby both feeding the grass and retaining moisture.

ithout regular precipitation, lawns need watering to stay soft and green. Even with watering, when summer sun is scorching hot for too long lawns tend to die off. This is why it is rare to see a healthy, green lawn outside of the temperate climate zone.

Hard landscaping, with terraces, paths, steps and statues, interspersed with containers brimming with plants are much more the Mediterranean style. Wildflower meadows and Zen gardens can provide other aesthetic alternatives to lawns. Gardens incorporating these styles can be artfully designed to create beautiful but quite different looking outside spaces from traditional temperate gardens with their large lawns surrounded by herbaceous borders.

If you feel you must keep your lawn despite the changing climate, then the following ideas are handy tips to maintain it.

Let go of the fantasy of a picture perfect, manicured, striped lawn; these take too many chemicals, too much water and back breaking work to maintain. Let the grass grow long as this provides more shade for the soil, thereby retaining some moisture. Reduce lawn size by creating paths, patios and terraces around the edges. Leave your lawn mowings in place as mulch, thereby both feeding the grass and retaining moisture.

GRASSES

During periods of hard drought the grass will turn brown. Although this is unsightly, you can leave it without watering, and when it rains eventually your lawn will spring back to life. If bare patches appear, try sowing in drought resistant grasses such as rye grass and Kentucky blue grass. From the organic perspective, lawns grown long without chemicals provide a good habitat for wildlife, and the ensuing wildflowers and weeds provide diversity.

WILDFLOWER MEADOWS

For those who cannot bear to live without a large expanse of grassy space in their garden, an ideal option is to transform your traditional lawn – or part of it – into a wildflower meadow. Sowing wildflower seeds directly into your existing lawn is unlikely to work. You need to first create the conditions for meadow grasses and wildflowers to thrive. Meadows do best in impoverished, subsoil with low fertility as this reduces competition from coarse weeds and strong plants, which prefer fertile topsoil.

To create a wildflower meadow, first dig out a patch or strip of your lawn turf together with the topsoil, and top up the space with subsoil. Rake through and firm the soil removing any large stones, then scatter a mixture of meadow grasses and wildflower seeds mixed with sand, rake in and firm the surface. The best time to plant your meadow is early autumn, as some seeds need the winter cold before germinating. You can also sow in mid-spring, although some species will not flower till the following year.

You can buy easily different mixes of wildflower and meadow grass seeds, such as for sunny or shady positions, all perennials or a mix of annuals and perennials. Or you can create your own mix. Start with several fine meadow grass species and then mix in your favourite wild flowers such as: poppies, cornflowers, field scabious, corn marigold, oxeye daisies, buttercups, trefoil, corn cockle, cowslips, yarrow, red vetch and so forth.

Maintaining your wildflower meadow does not involve much work. For a spring meadow, choose mainly plants that flower early, before mid-summer, so they set seed before cutting. Then cut mid to late summer after the seeds have dropped, using the resulting hay in your compost or as mulch. For a summer meadow, select later flowering species, and only cut down in mid-autumn. You can mow a summer meadow – with the blades of your mower set high – a couple of times in spring to encourage new growth.

HARD LANDSCAPING

Creating a visually pleasing garden that perhaps replaces a lawn using paving and terraces requires careful planning and design. We will consider hard landscaping designs, and look at some ideas for hard landscaping in the chapter on Mediterranean gardening.

This Japanese garden in The Hague, The Netherlands, provides an oriental calm

Zen Gardens

he traditional Japanese rock garden, known as a *karesansui*, has become known in the West as a Zen garden, or – in Japanese – a Zen *niwa*. Japanese gardens share simplicity of design with the careful arrangement of natural materials. According to the Japanese Shinto philosophy the garden symbolises the spiritual, sacred aspect of life, and provides a way to escape from the stresses of the mundane world.

Japanese Zen Buddhist philosophy regards the Zen garden as a microcosm of the entire universe. Swirls of raked gravel are symbolic of the rippling water of rivers and oceans; rocks and stones carefully placed amongst the raked gravel represent islands or mountains. The rocks are also thought to be the dwelling spaces of natural gods and spirits. Embellishments to the original sparse concept of Zen gardening, such as stepping-stones and stone lanterns, arose from the influence of the Japanese tea ceremony.

The simple but thoughtful designs of Zen gardens create a calming effect and provide a quiet place for meditation. Zen gardens are sometimes designed with an artfully placed seat.

A large Buddhist statue nestled amongst plants creates a tranquil atmosphere

This is so the garden can be viewed from a single perspective, providing the optimum vista to inspire tranquil reflection. A simple Zen style garden is easy to create, although there are specialists available who can design and build an authentic Zen garden for you.

A simple Zen garden might be an area of gravel, artfully raked into several swirling patterns evocative of water. Interspersed are a few irregularly shaped rocks of varying sizes, perhaps surrounded by moss, which can be arranged on a bed of white pebbles or sand. The gravel is supposed to be raked every day in a contemplative manner, creating new patterns as an object for meditation. You can place a small wooden bench nearby so you can meditate while contemplating the garden.

*Flowers and trees reflected in a lake add another dimension
to the garden*

CHAPTER 2

ATTRACTING WILDLIFE INTO YOUR GARDEN

Creating a wildlife-friendly garden is like having your own personal nature reserve at home that you can share with birds, insects and animals. Creating a garden that is friendly to and encouraging of wildlife does not mean letting your garden just run wild, although an untidy garden will attract wildlife. One good way to attract birds and animals to an ecological and friendly habitat that naturally provides food is to leave the tidying of borders and cutting back of shrubs till late winter or early spring. This delay supplies seeds, berries and fruit for birds and small mammals throughout winter, and also provides shelter for insects during the cold winter.

An overgrown corner of the garden provides a safe haven for this young fox. Photographed by John Gardner

Ladybirds eat greenfly and are welcome friends in the garden. Photographed by John Gardner

"By building up a wildlife community in the garden you will establish a balanced environment in which pests are less likely to get out of control."

(Pauline Pears & Sue Stickland)

Attracting Wildlife

Trees and wildflowers attract butterflies and help create an eco-friendly garden. Photographed by John Gardner

 wildlife garden can be both beautiful and a safe haven for birds, butterflies, insects and other 'garden friends'. Of course a wildlife garden is an organic garden, which means using no pesticides as these may deter or kill off the wildlife you wish to attract. However, the wildlife form part of the bio-diversity of the organic garden, and will eat most of the pests, thus rendering the undesirable pesticides redundant.

If you have a large garden then it is possible to imitate aspects of the natural wildlife habitats found amongst the woodlands, open glades, wetlands and grass lands of the countryside. For instance, butterflies love sheltered, sunny woodland glades. Planting a small group of birch or beech trees makes a small copse, creating a woodland habitat ideal for attracting butterflies.

The traditional, native species hedgerows, grown to divide up arable land into individual fields, provide vital food and shelter for a wealth of creatures. A small hedge can be easily incorporated into a modest sized garden – perhaps replacing an old fence. Hedges are useful as windbreaks and to define separate areas, or even to hide the compost heap. Such natural habitat features are a bonus for the wildlife in your garden, as well as being attractive all year round.

Even a small garden has enough space for a natural garden seat made from, perhaps, coppiced ash, which can be drilled with little holes for insects to occupy. Or a log pile, carefully arranged to give an attractive sculptural appearance, and that also provides an excellent home for beetles. Almost every garden can include some plants that produce fruit, berries and nutritious seeds to supplement the diet of birds and other wildlife.

Birds

here are many birds that are useful in the garden, although some can be a mixed blessing, such as blackbirds stealing fruit or sparrows pecking at seedlings and young flowers. However, thrushes will eat snails, first breaking their shells on a stone, and both blackbirds and thrushes eat caterpillars. Blue tits, great tits and sparrows eat aphids off plants, and starlings pecking in your lawn are probably searching for leatherjackets.

Ideally, an area for attracting birds would have nesting, roosting, feeding and watering places, although some birds will still visit a garden without these features. Sited away from the house, trees, hedges, shrubs and climbing plants are attractive as nesting places. Alternatively you can put up a nesting box. Choose a site for the nesting box that is fairly open, sheltered from winds and shaded from full sun.

A birdbath is valuable for birds in hot, dry summers both for drinking and bathing, and in winter for drinking, although you need to check daily that the water is not frozen. Most importantly to attract birds you need to provide a source of natural food. In deep winter you will need to put out extra food for birds such as peanuts, sunflower seeds and 'fat balls' – rounds of solid fat studded with seeds and nuts.

However, for most of the year you can provide a natural larder by growing flowers that attract insects and shrubs that produce berries. Leave the dead-heads on flowers that produce seeds, such as sunflowers, until the seed eating birds, such as gold and green finches, have stripped them bare.

Greenfinch searching for insects on a mossy tree branch.
Photographed by John Gardner

ATTRACTING WILDLIFE INTO YOUR GARDEN

Woodpeckers make nests in large trees. Photographed by John Gardner

A nest box for insects blends harmoniously into this garden

Other Wildlife

A baby hedgehog hiding behind a plant pot

lthough frogs and toads need ponds or similar water source for breeding and hibernation, they can be found in gardens without a pond, so long as there are damp, warm, shady conditions to shelter in. If you have a pond, then frogs and toads will be a familiar sight in your garden and they are major predators of slugs; toads also eat snails and ants.

Hedgehogs are night hunters, often travelling long distances in search of food, and not often seen in the daytime as they hide under hedges or large shrubs. They are very useful in the garden, eating a wide variety of pests, particularly slugs, millipedes and caterpillars. They are attracted by piles of leaves, thick, low hedges and large herbaceous shrubs and log piles.

Slowworms spend most of their time underground, but come out to bask in the warmth of the sun and to usefully eat slugs. They like compost heaps, stones, long grass and the borders between sun and shade.

BENEFICIAL INSECTS

Although some insects, like greenfly, are obviously undesirable, many other insects are of great benefit in the garden. Some insects, however, can be both friend and foe; for instance, earwigs will eat aphids but can also savage your prize dahlias. The best policy is to tolerate those insects that provide some benefit and to protect as necessary – or not grow in the first place – vulnerable plants.

Ladybirds are lovely and also useful, eating greenfly, small caterpillars and other pests. They like an untidy garden with old, dry plants, hollow stems and flaking bark to hibernate in. Hover flies look like small wasps, but with only one set of wings. Their larvae eat aphids and small caterpillars. Lacewings are green with delicate wings and also eat aphids, mites, leafhoppers and small caterpillars.

To attract hover flies and lacewings, grow open, small flowers that attract the insects with pollen and nectar. The old-fashioned varieties are best as these usually have single rather than double flowers, so they are much more accessible to insects seeking nectar and pollen. Good insect attracting flowering plants include: fennel, dill, angelica, sunflower, yarrow and Shasta daisies.

Bees and butterflies also favour herbs such as lavender, thyme and marjoram, and butterflies especially are attracted to buddleias, hebes and heliotropes. Bees are important for pollination and although caterpillars are a nuisance butterflies in the garden are delightful.

Ground beetles and centipedes are great garden friends as they both eat slugs, and centipedes also eat snails and other insects. They live in moist and shady soil, under stones, logs and piles of plant debris. They like an undisturbed habitat, and mulches and ground cover plants create suitable conditions for them.

As bees feed on nectar they help plants to pollinate
Photographed by John Gardner

Creating a Pond

There are many different kinds of ponds and water features available as they are currently fashionable in contemporary garden design. Although water features such as fountains and waterfalls can look most attractive and do encourage some forms of wildlife, nonetheless they can be wasteful of water – especially through evaporation when it's hot. Decorative water features are therefore not recommended in a green organic garden. However, ponds can be eco-friendly havens for wildlife and also look quite lovely so a wildlife pond makes a better choice for gardeners facing global warming and climate change.

There is potentially a suitable size pond for every garden, except for the smallest balcony or patio. If you have a large garden you can create a large pond, surrounded with lots of marginal plants and a profusion of floating water lilies on the surface. However, a large pond in a small garden can dominate everything else and look overwhelming and out of place. So, if you have a small garden, patio or terrace and you really want a pond then the best choice is a small pond or a container pond.

DIFFERENT TYPES OF PONDS

You can make a container pond in several different types of waterproof vessel. Particularly eye-catching are large stone bowls, which come in a variety of shapes and sizes. Ceramic pots can look attractive, but you need to check whether they are liable to crack or break if they remain filled with water over winter. Wooden barrels cut in half make good container ponds because they are large and durable and will not be damaged by winter frosts.

Small container ponds only hold a little water, so may become too hot for fish, wildlife or plants to survive in summer and will kill everything in a hard winter if they freeze over completely. Therefore it's best to site a small container pond out of direct sunlight, and to make sure you have plenty of oxygenating pond plants to help prevent algae forming. In winter, either move the pond under cover into a sheltered position, or drain the pond completely and keep any fish or plants in a bowl or tank of water in an unheated conservatory or greenhouse.

Other ponds start life as a hole dug into the ground, which is then usually lined with either concrete or butyl. An alternative is to dig a hole to the exact shape and size of a fibreglass shell, which is then fixed inside the hole. Also available are cheap PVC liners, but they don't last long and can't be repaired if they spring a leak. The best liner for a wildlife pond is butyl, as it is flexible, unobtrusive and durable.

"A water feature encourages wildlife, provides a home for plants with unusual and attractive flowers and foliage, and best of all, is tranquil and relaxing – a haven of peace in your garden."

(A TITCHMARSH, C DIMMOCK & T WALSH)

ATTRACTING WILDLIFE INTO YOUR GARDEN

42

Tips on Making a Pond

If you do not already have a pond in your garden, then you need to create a new pond.

- Work out what size of pond will best suit your garden. If you have a medium to large size garden then dig a hole for a pond in a suitable site.

- Avoid making a pond under trees to prevent too much shade and leaves falling in. If you want to fit a solar pump to aerate the water, then you need a sunny position.

- Decide on a vessel for a container pond, or purchase a butyl liner for an in-the-ground pond.

- Dig a hole and line your pond, or purchase a half wooden barrel or large stone bowl for your container pond.

- Try to avoid filling the pond from a mains water source as mains water contains many mineral salts that encourage algae. Instead, place lots of bowls and buckets around the garden and collect rainwater, or use rainwater already stored in your water butt.

- Plant water loving marginal plants such as iris, marsh marigold and flowering rush around the edges of an in-the-ground-pond.

- Plant pond plants in mesh sided containers filled with aquatic plant compost. Finish with a layer of fine gravel to prevent the compost floating away. Put some baskets on the base of the pond and some on shelves half way up the sides.

- Water lilies come in all sizes, even miniature ones for container ponds, and add a beautiful finishing touch to all ponds. There are a wide variety of colours ranging from deep red, through pastels to pure white.

- Make sure you include some oxygenating plants in your pond to keep the water clear and prevent algae or blanket weed from forming.

Creating A Wildlife Pond

You may be lucky and already have an established pond in your garden, and if you do it is easy to make it more wildlife friendly. If not, then you need to start from scratch and make a new pond that is attractive to wildlife. A wildlife pond not only encourages many different kinds of birds, animals and insects to visit your garden, but is also eco-friendly and low maintenance.

Although fish may be thought of as wildlife, they are in fact an introduced species and unfortunately they eat tadpoles and other small creatures. A pond with fish also requires more maintenance and interventions than a wildlife pond, so – although it is possible to have a large wildlife pond with a few fish – it is a good idea to go for lots of interesting plants instead of fish in your pond to encourage natural wildlife from the local habitat.

It is important to make at least one side of your pond a very gently sloping incline; try covering it with pebbles so you create a natural beach. You will soon see all types of birds and other wildlife coming to drink. Steep sided ponds allow animals such as hedgehogs to fall in and drown, and even frogs and toads can drown if they can't get out of a pond.

You can try to find some local frogspawn in spring and introduce a clump into your pond, but avoid bringing frogspawn in from a distance as this can spread disease. However, the best way to encourage all kinds of wildlife is to create a suitable environment and they will gradually appear. This means planting lots of marginal plants around the pond to give cover and attract insects. Avoid paving stones or concrete around the sides, and use small pebbles and natural stones instead.

Choose only native species of pond and marginal plants, and try to have as wide a variety as possible. You can use garden soil at the bottom of a wildlife friendly pond to plant deep aquatic plants, and use baskets on shelves half way up the sides for plants requiring less depth of water. Have lots and lots of plants. After a while you will be rewarded with newts, frogs and toads in the pond, dragonflies teeming above it, and hedgehogs coming to drink from the edges along with many different birds drinking and bathing.

ATTRACTING WILDLIFE INTO YOUR GARDEN

A garden chair on decking by a pond with water lilies provides a lovely place to sit and reflect

CHAPTER 3

THE DROUGHT RESISTANT GARDEN

Many drought-tolerant plants that are suitable for planting in the cooler temperate regions come from the Mediterranean countries. The normal climactic conditions in the Mediterranean are hot, dry summers and cool winters with little, or even no, frost; conditions in which many drought tolerant plants thrive. For plants from these regions to survive winter successfully in a temperate climate, you must select carefully only those varieties that are fully winter hardy, or be prepared to protect more vulnerable plants from frost.

Glass cloches protecting seedlings in spring from late frosts

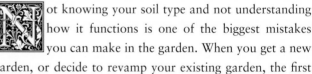

Soil Types

"*Many enthusiastic gardeners, anxious to be advised on what they shall plant, are floored by the simple question: What kind of soil do you have?*"

(BETH CHATTO)

Not knowing your soil type and not understanding how it functions is one of the biggest mistakes you can make in the garden. When you get a new garden, or decide to revamp your existing garden, the first thing to do is assess what type of soil you've got.

Begin by inspecting your flowerbeds. Pick up a handful of damp soil, squeeze it between your hands and feel and look at what you're holding. Does it feel gritty? Can you ball it into pliable shapes? This simple way to check your soil will determine its type. Serious gardeners can also use a soil testing kit to test the PH value.

WHAT IS SOIL?

The natural ground beneath our feet is basically soil, although for urban dwellers the only soil they may come across is the soil in their garden. The country dweller is surrounded by a lot more soil, but all gardeners need to assess carefully their soil type.

Understanding your soil type is essential to grow plants successfully

Soil is a mixture of broken up rock of different sizes and humus or rotted vegetation. The proportion of rock to humus and the size of the particles of rock help determine what type of soil you have. Listed below are the different soil types and suggestions on how to make the best of each.

GRAVEL & SANDY SOIL

As the name suggests, gravel soil contains lots of gravel, small stones and coarse grains. Sandy soil feels gritty and has much smaller, more uniform particles. Both these soils are free draining and don't hold water, so rain drains through almost instantly. They are consequently dry soils and drought is a big problem with these soil types.

To improve gravel and sandy soils you need to dig in lots of manure, compost and other humus. This improves the soils texture, nutrition for plants and ability to hold water. The positive side of sandy soil is that it is light and easy to work with and well aerated so plant roots spread well.

CLAY, LOAM & CHALK SOILS

The fine particles of clay soil ball easily into a solid, plastic mass, quite the opposite of sandy soil. Clay soil holds water only too well making it difficult and heavy to work with. Plant roots struggle to establish themselves. The answer once again is to incorporate a lot of compost, and also straw rich manure to lighten the texture and improve drainage.

If you are lucky you will have a loam soil, which is an ideal mixture of sandy and clay soils. Loam has sufficient clay to hold water and enough sand to allow aeration. Loam soil provides a good workable texture and needs less compost or manure dug in.

Chalk soil is naturally alkaline, thereby limiting the plants that will thrive in it. Often mixed with clay, chalk soil is difficult to work with and needs a lot of humus dug in to make a good garden soil.

Drought Resistant Garden: Ambience & Plants

Many gardeners accustomed to cool temperate climates have been adversely affected by the recent long, hot, dry summers brought about by the onset of global warming. However, it is important to remember that drought is a relative term. For the peoples of the drought stricken regions of Africa and Asia endemic drought is a much more awful reality than our dry summers and hose pipe bans. For them the failure of the annual rains and the resulting shrivelled crops is life threatening.

If we choose to help, we can donate to drought crisis appeals and support charities that work in these areas, but it is important also to adapt our lifestyles accordingly. Creating a drought tolerant garden in which water is treated as a precious resource and not mindlessly wasted is an ethical response to the worldwide dilemma of increasing water scarcity.

There are a surprisingly wide variety of drought tolerant plants. These range from those capable of dealing with very arid, desert like conditions to those more suited to the less challenging conditions of semi-desert, and include some plants native to Europe. Many of these plants have flourished in the long, hot, dry summers of late, and – because desert climates often have very cold spells as well as hot – they need little or no frost protection.

Obviously the main feature of drought tolerant plants is their ability to survive with little and infrequent input of water, but what are the other characteristics of drought tolerant plants?

How Plants Manage Drought

Since the beginning of vegetation on this planet millions of years ago, plants have been evolving to cope with the different, sometimes hostile conditions they encounter. Most notable are plants that come in the category of 'silvers and greys', such as mugwort, sagebrush, cotton lavender, artemisia, cinerarias and wormwood. These have fine hairs all over their leaves, which act as a defence against the drying effects of wind and sun.

Other plants protect themselves with leaves that have a waxy outer coating, whilst succulents such as agaves have rigid fleshy leaves and toothed edges, often tipped with sharp spines. A few plants have evolved in such a way as to have minimized or dispensed with leaves altogether to reduce moisture loss.

A broad range of drought tolerant plants exists to select from when considering making your garden more eco-friendly. Some of these will be considered in more detail in the chapters on tropical and exotic, and Mediterranean gardens.

For instance, plants as diverse as the periwinkle creeping along the flower bed with its trailing leaves and bright blue flowers, and the stately bush ceanothus that bursts into masses of blue flowers in spring are both drought resistant, familiar favourites in the temperate garden. Also several varieties of the beautiful and hardy aquilegia, such as Dragonfly, the ubiquitous potentillas that produce their yellow or orange flowers in summer and the stately bay tree are equally familiar and drought tolerant.

"You can often tell whether a plant will be drought resistant by its appearance."

(Charlotte Green)

Aloe, Agave, and Grass Tree planted together create a tropical ambience

Golden Cinquefoil is a hardy, drought resistant plant

Rocks, gravel and trees blend together harmoniously in this Japanese garden in Germany

> *"Some basic principles of design can be employed in any garden, but it's important first to recognize the need for a design."*
>
> (ANDY STURGEON)

Drought Resistant Garden: Planning & Design Tips

When you feel ready to plan and design your drought resistant garden, the first step is to consider what you actually have. Soil type – and how best to deal with what you've got – has already been considered. A good next step is to take some photographs of your existing garden space. Ideally take photos of the same view over a number of months so you can consider what the garden looks like over the different seasons.

Examine all the photographs and identify any weak spots, and things you want to change. For instance, you might want to do away with the lawn to lessen watering. You then decide that you would like to install a wildflower meadow, or perhaps a Zen garden with raked gravel. Look at lots of pictures of what you think you would like. Also visit many different gardens that include these features; it's a pleasurable way to find inspiration and help you reach a decision.

Consider your garden as a living three-dimensional sculpture that changes throughout the seasons. You create different shapes with plants and structures, and understanding how they relate to each other is key to good garden design. A useful tip is to choose one basic shape – such as a curve, circle or square – and then echo this one shape with slight variations throughout the garden. This gives an aesthetically pleasing cohesive style to the garden.

For a drought resistant garden, you'll want to incorporate some kind of windbreak, dividing the garden into separate 'rooms' to slow the wind's path and ameliorate its drying effect. If your garden is small, then panels of trellis with lots of climbing plants is effective. This design also allows wind to gust through the gaps, so even a strong wind is unlikely to blow the trellis over. Hedges are a good alternative for a larger garden and encourage wildlife. Many hedging plants are both attractive and drought resistant.

DRAWING PLANS

Next make a simple plan of your garden plot. Measure the boundaries and draw the garden shape to working scale; for instance in a medium sized garden use a centimetre to a metre. Mark on your plan anything you can't change such as the location of the house, features like garden sheds and ponds, plus any trees or plants you want to keep.

Make several copies of the plan for scribbling down ideas, and generally working towards your new garden design. Try out different locations for a new patio, Zen garden or hedge and see how they might work in terms of the overall design of the garden. Remember to include a space for a compost heap or bin. Start thinking about which drought resistant plants you want to include, and where they might be planted.

Make sure you are completely happy with your design plan before you actually start. Once you've begun to dig up your lawn it becomes difficult to deviate successfully from the original plans. Start with the major work first, such as removing turf, erecting a trellis or planting a hedge. Then incorporate new features, such as bringing in gravel to make a Zen garden, and finally plant out new plants.

Gravel is raked into swirling patterns evocative of water in this Zen garden

Large Garden Project

For the large drought resistant garden project we will consider and review a real life project planned, designed and planted by Sara Jane Rothwell of Glorious Gardens. The original garden was a pretty basic affair as you can see from the 'before' photo below. It consisted mainly of a large lawn with a group of mature beech trees at the end away from the house, with bushes and shrubs to one side and untended bare soil, ivy and a few straggly self seeded young trees to the other side. Developing this simple, unstructured space into a well designed, low maintenance, environmentally friendly and drought tolerant garden posed an exciting challenge.

 o begin with, some basic construction and erection of new boundary fences was required to better define the garden space. The decision was made to opt for one-meter high oak posts, spaced out at 2.5 m gaps, with three rows of tensioned galvanized wire strung between the posts. This provides a long lasting and durable fence. Because of the large size and woodland nature of the garden already providing natural screening, privacy was not considered a major issue, so the open style of the fencing was not a problem. In addition, new green oak was purchased from a local supplier for the construction of the terraced retaining walls and the arbour.

Obviously the beautiful mature beech trees seen in the 'before' photo would remain as a central feature, but careful consideration was needed to decide how to work round them. Firstly, as mature trees they were tall and caused a great deal of shade, which affects and limits what can be planted nearby. Secondly, it is very difficult to grow most plants under beech trees, so this affected how the immediate surrounding areas were planned and designed. However,

as can be seen from the 'after' photo on the right, the more formally designed and planted areas segue naturally and harmoniously into the less developed woodland area around and under the beech trees.

The finished garden as shown in the after photo above has a contemporary feel, with a clever mix of formal plantings integrated with natural woodland areas.

A large garden such as this must rely to some extent on physically powerful structural design and architectural plants, and here the beech trees give a strong focal point. Combined with interesting surfaces such as the bark mulch, a wide variety of different plants, and features such as the terraced beds and arbour the overall impression of the garden is one of Nature in harmony with human design.

GREEN CREDENTIALS

The garden was designed to be environmentally friendly, drought tolerant and low maintenance. The photo at the bottom of this page shows two key green features. Firstly you can see the fenced area providing space for two compost bins – this is the best way to compost with one bin undergoing the composting process with the bottom layer just about ready for use while the other bin is built up with fresh vegetable peelings, grass clippings and so forth. The bins finally were installed once the planting and all the other gardening work was completed.

Secondly, you can see the thick bark mulch covering all of the surface area of the beds around the plants. Not only does this minimise moisture loss and make the best use of rainfall, but the mulch has been also applied quite thickly to discourage any but the most persistent weeds. With very few weeds having a chance to grow through, the amount of time spent weeding is much reduced. In this way, the natural state of the garden is undisturbed much of the time – encouraging wildlife to visit – and the soil structure is not broken down by repeatedly walking over it.

CHOICE OF PLANTS

Plants were chosen for their suitability for the soil type and other of the garden's conditions such as sunlight, shade, exposure and so forth. Plants were also selected for their individual aesthetic qualities and for their ability to combine harmoniously into the garden as a whole. The natural, woodland style of the garden has been enhanced by a choice of plants that blend well together. Whilst some more formal, highly stylised or cottage gardens can take lots of different colours and flowers, the more natural feel of this garden is highlighted by keeping to mainly different shades of green with some white flowers and grasses.

One of the few exceptions is the pretty and dramatic red flowers that you can see have been carefully and generously interspersed amongst the other plants. This plant is the lovely penstemon garnet, or Penstemon Andenken an Friedrich Hahn. Penstemon garnet is a bushy semi-evergreen perennial that can grow up to 90cm in height, so the bright flowers

are easily visible both above and through the other plants. Its narrow, dark green leaves help show off the bell-shaped, deep wine-red flowers, accented with white on the throat of the petals. Generally disease free, penstemon garnet tolerates almost all soil types and aspects so it fits in well to the garden's natural, low maintenance, drought tolerant remit.

The penstemons are particularly complemented by the Mexican feather grass, or Texas needle grass (stipa tenuissima). The close up detail photo (above) of the grass covered with dew shows the pretty, almost luminous shades of green and white colours of the grass, and perhaps this variegation gave rise to its other common name of ponytails. This deciduous grass has narrow, arching, feathery flowers of pale brown and pale green in summer. Ponytails is a hardy, easy to care for plant ideally suited to this garden.

1. Retaining walls constructed with new oak sleepers have been used on the sloping area here to create terraces. Terracing helps prevent heavy rains washing away topsoil and young plants, and creates small, flat planting areas.

12. The attractive 'ponytails' forms a compact, upright tuft of thread-like leaves, delicate, feathery flowers in summer, and is a typical, hardy, low maintenance grass.

11. This easy to grow grass is a great plant that tolerates all conditions and aspects. Purple moor grass gets its name from the purple flowers in summer that contrast well with the foliage that turns yellow in autumn.

10. Lady's mantle is a familiar sight in wildflower and woodland gardens. Particularly well sited on banks and slopes, lady's mantle often self seeds freely to form informal groups in the surrounding area.

9. The dramatic and outstanding penstemon garnet has won an award of garden merit. An easy to establish semi-evergreen perennial, penstemon garnet takes up to five years to reach its ultimate height and full potential.

8. The low maintenance tussock sedge (carex flagellaris) is often used in prairie plantings. As an evergreen perennial, this grass has year round interest and it fits well into a mixed border such as this one.

7. With no pruning required the easy growing perennial Dicentra spectabilis 'Alba' is maintenance free. However, care must be taken with this plant as the foliage may aggravate skin allergies, and all parts may cause stomachache if eaten.

2. Statuesque mature beech trees create a focal point that draws attention. Although difficult for many plants to flourish under them, the beeches lessen to some extent the effects of wind and provide year round interest as the leaves change colour.

3. Arbours are useful structural features, and work especially well in large gardens as they do not dominate their surroundings. Constructed of local green oak, the arbour has young climbing plants trained to gradually grow up it.

4. These delicate stems with branched clusters of small, purple flowers are verbena bonariensis, commonly known as purple top, Argentinian vervain, South American vervain, or tall verbena. This tall perennial can reach up to 2 m in height.

6. This bushy perennial is Gaura lindheimeri, or white gaura. Its slender erect stems bear small spoon-shaped leaves and prolific starry white or pink-tinged flowers in summer and autumn. Happy in all aspects it is typical of prairie planting.

5. Its drought resistant and low maintenance attributes makes acanthus mollis well suited to this garden. Also known as bear's breech, this vigorous plant with large, glossy dark green leaves, bears tall white flowers with dusky purple bracts in late summer.

CHAPTER 4

THE TROPICAL & EXOTIC GARDEN

Tropical plants look dramatically different from typical temperate plants and they create a spectacular new look for the garden. These exotic plants thrive and look best planted amongst natural stones, with features such as raked gravel areas – perhaps a small Zen garden – and sandy, gravel or flagstone paths. As long as the individual plants are chosen carefully with regard to hardiness, then a tropical exotic garden can be made in cooler, temperate regions quite easily.

"Make sure that any plant you choose for a particular spot in your garden is going to like it there. Does the plant do best in sun or shade? Plants that are put in the wrong place will never thrive and are more susceptible to pest and disease attack."

(PAULINE PEARS & SUE STICKLAND)

Agave and Aloe, flouring in the Jardim Botânico, Madeira, Portugal

Sun & Shade

nce upon a time gardeners thought a shady north-facing garden meant not being able to grow many flowering plants. A sunny, south or southwest facing aspect was considered essential for a successful flower garden. However, in recent years many more shade tolerant plants have become available, so having a shady garden now offers the opportunity to get to know a whole new category of plants.

In the face of global warming, some shade in the garden is now becoming welcome to increasingly more plants – as it is to the gardeners who tend them. Perhaps surprisingly, there are quite a few tropical and exotic plants that do well in partial shade, for instance tree ferns and slipper plants (calceolaria), so even without a south-facing aspect you can create a tropical exotic ambience. A big plus is that fewer weeds tend to spring up in shady aspects because lack of sunlight inhibits germination.

All plants have specific sun exposure requirements, a key bit of information you need to know before buying new plants. Equally important is to be aware of how much sun and shade your garden has – especially for a small garden with little space to play with. This information then helps you decide which plants are suitable for your garden.

A mature Japanese Maple provides dappled shade in a park

SUN EXPOSURE TERMINOLOGY

A plant labelled as requiring full sun means it needs at least 6 full hours of direct sunlight a day to do well. A sunny south or southwest facing aspect may enjoy more than 6 hours at the height of summer, and you should remember that even tropical exotic plants there might need a little extra watering to endure the heat.

Partial sun/partial shade means the plant needs between 3–6 hours of sun each day, preferably in the morning and early afternoon. Dappled sunlight is similar to partial sun/partial shade, but refers to the sunlight that filters through the branches of a deciduous tree. Woodland plants prefer this type of sunlight.

Full Shade means plants that like less than 3 hours of direct sunlight each day, preferably with some filtered sunlight during the rest of the day. Full shade does not mean no sun at all as there are few plants, except mushrooms, that can survive in the dark.

TYPES OF SHADE

The degree of shade in your garden will change with the season and time of day. Spend time during different seasons watching when and where the light and shadows fall in your garden and consider this when planning new plantings.

Deciduous trees throw dappled shade through their leaves from late spring through summer. If they are blocking out too much sun then remove some of the lower branches to allow more sunlight through. However, there is little to be done with buildings that cast shade over your garden.

If you want to create more shade then it is easy to erect simple structures. Pergolas, trellis, arches and arbours covered with climbers can all be used to cast dappled shade onto specific areas.

"There is nothing quite like a stunning tropical climber amongst summer bedding or growing up a warm house wall. They always bring happy memories of holidays and their sheer exuberance and rampant growth can be surprising even in our lukewarm summers."

(Peter White)

The Tropical & Exotic: Ambience & Plants

Going on a sunny winter holiday to a hot, tropical location used to create impossible dreams for many gardeners of bringing back some of the wonderful exotic plants they had seen growing there, and transplanting them into their more temperate gardens back home. However, with global warming and subsequent climate change bringing warmer, drier weather to many previously cold and damp places, these dreams can now be realised.

Tropical and exotic gardens can take two main different approaches. The first style of tropical exotic gardening – often practised by those who already live in a hot, dry region – is to create a personal oasis of lush greenery, colourful foliage and exotic flowers amongst arid desert like surroundings. If this scheme holds particular appeal for you then you must first turn your mind to drought tolerant plants that require minimal water to hold true to the principle of adapting ethically to climate change.

Green Fingers Tip

To make the most of these plants, these exotics are best sited in a small group in an area of the garden, such as on the patio, where you will see them frequently and can enjoy them to the full.

Large tropical plants adorn the Cascade Garden in the Botanic Gardens, Singapore

Ideally, select mainly drought tolerant plants for your tropical exotic garden to provide screening, shade and ground cover. Then you can treat yourself to a few lush, green, water-demanding tropical plants with large, bold coloured flowers that can be accommodated in pots, or perhaps small flowerbeds with underground irrigation systems. To make the most of these plants, these exotics are best sited in a small group in an area of the garden, such as on the patio, where you will see them frequently and can enjoy them to the full.

CREATING A DESERT AMBIENCE

Another approach to tropical exotic gardening is to try to accentuate the hot, dry conditions of the desert ambience. You can embrace the fact that global warming is bringing about climate change quite rapidly, and revel in these challenging new gardening conditions. A desert style tropical garden typically includes plants such as spiky yuccas, prickly pear and agaves.

To create an interesting overall effect with your tropical garden, you need to consider a variety of different plants, including large spreading palms to give structure and shade, and to provide a contrast with spiky cactus and other small plants. The cycads are particularly interesting to consider here. This fascinating group of plants looks a bit like both palms and ferns yet belongs to neither family. The broad fronds of cycads radiate outwards and make a bold impression.

Perhaps the most well known of the tropical exotic plants is the Canary island date palm. This palm will be familiar to everyone who has travelled to warmer climes where it is almost ubiquitous. Growing eventually to quite a tall height, the Canary island date palm creates a strong visual effect in the sunshine with dappled bright light and dark shadows contrasting spectacularly with bright sunlight. Plants that do require some shade and protection from hot sun can be planted nearby where the palms throw shade.

"Extravagantly waving fronds, outrageously gaudy blossoms, palms hung with fruit & exotic plants have become horticulture's hottest item. They're even coming out of the greenhouse and into the garden as people see how simple it is to grow colourful bougainvillea, tree ferns, hibiscus and more."

(PETER WHITE)

The dramatic large flowers Hibiscus Rose of China flower freely in Gran Canaria, Spain

The Tropical & Exotic: Planning & Designing Tips

When planning and designing a tropical, exotic garden you need to make the most of the sun the garden receives and the heat it radiates. Ideally you need a protected garden without exposed areas to avoid frost and wind damage. For instance, having – or building – a south or southwest facing wall will block out chilling and drying wind, creating a mild micro-climate. Plant tropical exotic plants in the shelter of this wall, or train climbers against it. The bricks hold onto the heat for hours after the sun has gone down.

Hard landscaping makes for an authentic tropical look in the garden, but is useful too. Like the south-facing wall above, brick and stone borders and paths act like storage radiators, holding and slowly releasing heat overnight. In this way delicate, non-hardy exotic plants have their best chance of survival planted alongside any form of hard landscaping that receives sunlight.

One design tip that works especially well in a tropical exotic garden is to build some steps using large slabs of natural stone. Not only can you plant delicate cultivars alongside, but also even a small change in level emphasises the different dimensions of the garden, creating visual interest. Steps encourage movement within the whole garden space and create a vista that naturally leads the eye down the garden to enjoy all the different plants and features.

PLANNING THE TROPICAL EXOTIC LOOK

Many exotics are tougher than their reputations suggest, so be bold and experiment with the tropical plants that take your fancy. A wide range of tropical plants are now available so you can create a simple low maintenance tropical exotic garden, or introduce plants that need a lot more care and attention.

A profusion of Bougainvillea blossoms are a familiar sight in tropical countries

A simple way to enjoy the tropical exotic look is to choose and purchase the plants you want – regardless of hardiness – and plant them out in containers. When winter approaches you can either bring the plants into a conservatory or greenhouse, or let them take their chances. Some will doubtless die, but a few may surprise you by re-appearing the following spring.

You can of course protect tropical plants by wrapping plant fleece around the whole plant, or cover with straw at the base. For plants such as ginger lilies that have rhizomatous roots, let the plant die back naturally then heap piles of soil over the roots; if the mounds are sufficiently large then the rhizomes will not freeze and die.

Tropical exotic plants typically include big, spiky cactus, banana plants with large unusual shaped leaves, palms with massive fronds, and climbers such as bougainvillea with masses of colourful flowers. Artistically grouped together, they create living sculptures in your borders.

Green Fingers Tip

Plant tropical exotic plants in the shelter of a sunny wall, or train climbers against it. The bricks hold onto the heat for hours after the sun has gone down.

Browse through exotic plant catalogues looking for plants you like and decide what will look good together and suit your garden conditions. Then start ordering, but avoid the temptation to choose too many different varieties, as this creates a busy, crowded feel. Try halving the number of different plants you want and doubling the quantities.

> *With careful selection and planning, a small garden can give pleasure and interest all year round."*
>
> (BETH CHATTO)

The Tropical & Exotic: Small Garden Project

The small garden project to create a tropical, exotic garden described here is designed to be easy to establish, quick to get going and low maintenance. This simple and adaptable plan provides an easy place to start tropical exotic gardening and should not be overly daunting to the keen amateur gardener. Although you may fancy the ambience and look of a full blown tropical exotic garden you may not have the ideal aspect and other conditions in your own garden, so the project below includes mainly hardy varieties of tropical exotic plants.

The idea of dealing with too many unfamiliar, delicate, non-hardy and expensive tropical cultivars may be intimidating, especially if you do not have access to either a conservatory or a greenhouse for over-wintering your plants. These wonderful foreign exotics tend to be more expensive than native varieties and the cost of replacing these plants, should they succumb to a hard frost, can be prohibitive. So a good place to begin tropical exotic gardening and gain some experience is start with the hardier plants to give you the best chance of success.

There are quite a few herbaceous perennials and annuals that appear more exotic than in fact they actually are. They all create a tropical exotic ambience, but also cope with adverse climactic conditions such as long, hard winters. In the overall scheme of the garden plan, these plants combine well with hardy varieties of palms and cycads giving an overall tropical exotic impression, but in fact being surprisingly tough and resilient.

CONSIDERING THE GARDEN SPACE

As we are looking at a small garden project here, the first thing to establish is whether your garden is small, or whether perhaps you have a large garden and wish to create a separate tropical exotic 'room' within the overall garden space. If you are lucky enough to have a large garden and are looking to create a tropical exotic zone, then you have the luxury of being able to choose the best site. In this case you would select the most sheltered area of the garden, typically with a south or southwest aspect.

However, the majority of people live in towns and cities these days, and the typical urban garden is in most instances a small space. This means you must make the best of what you have, but even a north facing, shady garden will have a few sunny, sheltered spots that can be used for hardy tropical exotics. Remember all aspects include a south, or southwest, facing border.

An autumn garden full of color in afternoon sunshine

Landscaping

As you have read earlier, some form of hard landscaping is needed in a tropical exotic garden to help create the right ambience and to retain the sun's heat. Hard landscaping should be considered first, because once it's in place it's hard work to change. Look at your garden and establish if you already have paving, bricks or perhaps a concrete patio. Decide whether you want to keep what you have or whether you would like to change or add new hard surfaces.

 ssuming you want to incorporate some new hard landscaping into your garden, the first decision to make is which materials to use. Ideally you want to remain sympathetic to your surroundings by choosing similar or complementary materials rather than choosing something that will clash with what is already in place.

Take a good look around your immediate surroundings and consider the walls and roofs of your and neighbouring houses, the local paving materials, and any naturally occurring stone. This will give you an idea of what materials will work best. As you are working in a small garden choose just one or two to prevent a crowded, messy look.

The easiest material to work with is gravel. You can create a simple but authentic tropical exotic garden look with gravel surfaces of two to three inches thick with soil underneath. Planting tropical exotic looking plants such as prickly pears, agaves, yuccas, cacti and echeverias into gravel creates a

quick, low cost striking effect. The thick gravel mulch prevents weeds springing up and drains effectively, which suits these plants.

This planting scheme creates an arid, desert feel, which can be softened if desired by including some delicate, feathery ornamental grasses. For instance, cloud grass provides a romantic haze of silver followed with pink flowers, and

Steps and a curved stone path naturally lead the eye deep into the garden

barley grass has eye-catching foliage. Site where the plants will receive full or partial sun both for the plants to thrive and because this scheme looks best in bright sunshine when it makes the most of the hot dry conditions.

To provide structure and clean design try enclosing gravel inside bricks or paving stones – or use recycled granite cobbles, obtainable from a reclaim yard – to create small beds or borders. This takes more preparatory work. To prevent design mistakes, you must first draw plans to scale on paper to develop the shape and size of the desired scheme before starting the actual physical work.

Curved, circular and angular shapes – such as square or rectangular – designs can all work well with this scheme; the choice is down to personal taste.

Giant Feather Grass adds a whimsical note to this shady garden

This Modjadji Cycad creates a striking focal point

Designing the Small Tropical Exotic Garden

Once you have sorted out your hard landscaping, it's time to consider and design the rest of the garden to continue the tropical exotic theme. It's important to create a focal point that can be enjoyed from the house. This might perhaps be a circular gravel bed surrounded by bricks in the centre of the garden, containing desert ambient plants, as described above. Alternatively, a large dramatic palm, tree fern, banana tree or cycad can also create a striking focal point in a small garden.

A Canary Island date palm can be grown in a bed or large container. Although not completely hardy, it does well in mild, sheltered areas if protected in winter, or can be grown in a container and moved inside. Mature palms produce beautiful bunches of cream, bowl-shaped flowers in summer, followed by edible fruit.

The Chinese hardy banana musa bajoo is a striking architectural plant, tall and slender with big bright green leaves. Or try a cycad; cycas revoluta, the sago palm, tolerates drought and is reputed to be hardy to − 9 °C. If you want to plant in shade, try a tree fern; dicksonia antartica is hardy to − 5 °C. Perhaps the easiest fully hardy palm is trachycarpus fortunei. It has an elegant shape, is drought tolerant and can be planted in the ground or a container.

The spread of a large palm is substantial in a small space, so plant shade tolerant plants underneath. Several ginger

74

A mixed group of hostas complemented by stone paving and seating

Green Fingers Tip

A simple design tip is to look from an upstairs window down on to your garden. This gives you a very different vista from the view you have in your garden and may inspire some creative ideas.

cultivars, such as cautleya gracilis, do well in shade and are hardy; this one produces gorgeous light yellow flowers August to September. Scan the plant catalogues for other tropical exotic under planting ideas, or even try traditional shade tolerant temperate plants such as hostas and ferns, impatiens and begonias. A flowering climber can be planted to thread through the fronds of a palm for a jungle effect.

A simple design tip is to look from an upstairs window down on to your garden. This gives you a very different vista from the view you have in your garden and may inspire some creative ideas. Ideally come up with a design that works well both when you are in the garden and when you look down at the view from the house.

Creating different levels helps to make a small garden feel larger. Stone steps draw the eye towards a focal point and creative use of mirrors, perhaps sited behind a large plant, increases the sense of space. A panel of trellis with a partially hardy exotic climber is simple and effective, but site carefully in a sunny sheltered position. For instance the passionflower passiflora allardi has a long flowering season of beautifully scented purple flowers. Passiflora racemosa has pretty purple flowers, or campsis madame galen has large red orange flowers. An easy climber is jasmine, which looks exotic, smells wonderful and is fully hardy.

FILLING THE GAPS

Once the hard landscaping and focal point have been established together with features such as mirrors and trellis with climbers, there remain gaps in the borders and on the patio. If you have a conservatory you can complete the tropical exotic look with a few pot plants that can over-winter inside; for instance, the spectacular bird of paradise, strelitzia reginae.

Hardy exotics can be planted in the beds and borders. Read the descriptions of each hardy tropical exotic you like in the catalogues first to see how big they will grow, and only purchase those you know you have plenty of room for. ***Try:***

- Hibiscus syriacus are fully hardy shrubs with large tropical flowers; hybrids are available in pink, purple blue and white.

- Planted in a sheltered position near a wall, hibiscus galaxy has huge flowers in pink, white or red.

- For pretty lilac blue flowers in spring try abutilon suntense which grows quickly and is fully hardy.

- Photinia red robin has spectacular spring red foliage turning to green bronze. Try planting a few together as a small hedge.

- Blue lyme grass is a broad leaved fully hardy grass, best in a pot to prevent it spreading.

CHAPTER 5

THE MEDITERRANEAN GARDEN

Mediterranean gardens are delightfully fragrant, conjuring up evocative memories with aromatic herbs and perfumed flowers. Reminiscent of the hot sun and blue sea, the scents of the Mediterranean garden inspire relaxation and tranquillity, inviting you to spend time enjoying your garden at leisure. Place a comfortable seat amongst the profusion of fragrant plants for scented inspiration on a sunny afternoon, and read a book, pull out your sketchbook or just lie back and daydream.

> *"Tiles are colourful and evocative of hot climates. Although Spanish and Moroccan tiles can be sealed to protect them from frost, it is better to search out look a likes, such as frost proof Italian tiles."*
>
> (SHIRLEY-ANNE BELL)

Garden Furniture, Ornaments & Accessories

 arden furniture needs careful consideration so that it fits in well with the ambience and style of your garden. This is particularly important for small gardens, especially a courtyard with plants in containers, as garden furniture can dominate such a small space unless carefully chosen and sited. For a Mediterranean garden the best options for garden furniture are hardwood or metal as these are traditionally used in sunny Mediterranean countries. Canvas and plastic furniture is cheap and cheerful, but may not suit the classic Mediterranean style. Wicker looks great, but has to come inside if it rains.

Hardwood is an increasingly popular choice, but needs to be sourced from a supplier who supports tree conservation and replanting schemes. Otherwise you will unwittingly be contributing to deforestation – one of the causes of global warming. Wood can be varnished or oiled every couple of years, or left to weather to a natural silvery-grey, which suits the Mediterranean ambience. However, unvarnished wood stays wet for ages after rain. Choose delicate rather than chunky designs, or your furniture may look too bulky and dominate a small garden.

Metal comes in a wide variety of styles ranging from contemporary to classical and can complement well the Mediterranean look. Traditional pieces made from cast iron are attractive and ornamental, although can be substantial and heavy, and rust if not painted or galvanised. Aluminium is lighter and needs less maintenance. Metal furniture is usually perforated and dries quickly after rain.

ORNAMENTS & ACCESSORIES

A Mediterranean container garden needs ornamentation to complement the style. Pale pastel coloured painted walls, especially blue, create a Mediterranean feel and brighten up the space, as well as giving plants extra reflected sunlight. Tiles and mosaics on walls and floor also make the space feel Mediterranean and are attractive and stylish, although they take extra work and cost more than painting. The beautiful and colourful patterns of traditional tiles – if you are lucky enough to find some – really do evoke the relaxed sunny Mediterranean mood.

You can create a focal point in your garden using accessories in several ways. For instance, a carefully placed object such as a statue will always catch the eye. For a Mediterranean ambience, choose classically designed statuary such as an urn or Greek style figurine. Too many objects can ruin the effect in a small space so a good design tip is to choose one really striking piece.

An *étagère* – a three-tiered metal rack for plant pots either shaped to fit in a corner or along a wall – is visually striking, especially with some bright coloured trailing plants. By using the vertical dimension of height as well as horizontal space, an *étagère* increases the amount of space for container plants. Solar lights look dramatic and give a soft diffused light for summer evenings, as well as being ecological. Try sticking them in pots alongside plants for a subtle lighting effect amongst the foliage.

A classically designed fountain sculpture creates a focal point in this pond in Mallorca

The Mediterranean Garden – Ambience & Plants

When we think of Mediterranean gardens and the idea of creating one for ourselves we tend to imagine dazzling, bright sunlight, vibrant coloured flowers and aromatic herbs and bushes. For many people a picture may arise of a walled courtyard or open terrace with large terracotta pots.

Perhaps you visualize a profusion of climbing plants scrambling up a wall, or imagine a formal large garden with olive trees, terraces and pathways. Mosaics and tiles, sandy paths, statuesque cypress trees, ornamental grasses, exotic bougainvillea blossoms can all spring to mind according to your personality. These different visions of the Mediterranean reveal how diverse this gardening style can be.

Typical Mediterranean Garden Characteristics

The Mediterranean garden thrives in areas that have hot, almost completely dry summers and mainly cool, sunny, wet winters. Countries such as Corsica, Sardinia, the Balearics and Sicily have Mediterranean climates with annual mean rainfall of around 879 mm and temperature of 17.2 °C.

Perhaps surprisingly, some Mediterranean countries can have brief spells of winter cold as low as −6 °C. This suggests that with a little extra protection, such as wrapping in straw or garden fleece, even non-frost tolerant plants from the Mediterranean have a good chance of survival in temperate countries as temperatures slowly warm up from global warming.

Some tender drought resistant Mediterranean plants have already been grown successfully alongside temperate varieties in milder regions and coastal areas. For instance, you might consider planting Astelia chathamica 'silver spear', which has wonderful sword shaped leaves with a metallic silver finish, somewhat reminiscent of a phormium. This is a great plant for growing in a shady corner and is hardy to −5 °C.

A typical Mediterranean garden will not have a lawn, as most temperate lawn grasses cannot survive the hot dry summers. If having a lawn is important to you, there are creative alternatives to traditional lawn grasses, such as creeping juniper and chamomile plus all the other suggestions from Chapter One.

Many ornamental grasses thrive in hot sunny conditions, and although not suitable to grow as a lawn, nonetheless often feature and do well in a Mediterranean garden. Instead of lawns, stone patios and terraces often with steps, walls and paths are typical. With careful plan and design they can look equally attractive as a lawn – and are a lot easier to maintain as well as not using up lots of water.

The Mediterranean garden features a lot of container planting with less herbaceous borders and flowerbeds. This is largely because containers use less water overall than in-the-ground planting, although depending on what kind of plants and containers you choose, watering may need to be fairly frequent. Another reason for the prevalence of container planting is that Mediterranean soil is typically poor, and compost can be easily added to containers to enrich the soil if required for particular plants.

Garden furniture and plants mingle harmoniously in this small space

"Although establishing a Mediterranean-style garden in a temperate area sounds challenging, it doesn't have to be."

(SHIRLEY-ANNE BELL)

This climbing hydrangea needs a strong trellis to support its weight

An informal planting of foxgloves, cranesbills and siberian iris surround an urn

> *"A small garden doesn't have to mean small pots. In fact large pots and plants in a small garden will create much more drama and impact than having everything below eye level."*
>
> (Joe Swift)

The Mediterranean Garden – Planning & Design

Before beginning to plan and design, spend some time reflecting on what you think your ideal Mediterranean garden might look like. From the images that form in your imagination from memories and garden books, you can start to select styles, themes, colours and individual plants that you would like to include. Although sharing some common characteristics, there are several different types of Mediterranean garden. So it's worth spending enough time, reflection and research in the early stages to ensure you end up with the garden of your dreams.

As you sit there daydreaming of the Mediterranean, try making notes of things you definitely would like to include, and those that you don't wish to have, in your garden. This is also the time to be practical; there's no point dreaming of a vast, rambling wilderness overlooking the sea when you have a small suburban courtyard to start with. However, there will always be a particular style and specific plants that can be incorporated into your garden whatever its size to help you realise a Mediterranean design.

You might also want to grow herbs and other plants which need different soil conditions from those you naturally have in your garden. Raised beds and especially containers are useful for these plants, as you can create any soil conditions you want in them.

FORMAL & INFORMAL MEDITERRANEAN STYLES

There is a long history of the formal Mediterranean style of gardening that draws from both 14th-century Renaissance garden design and the Moorish influence of Islamic gardens. Both these formal styles have the practical aspect of providing shade from the relentless summer sun of the Mediterranean climate by including shady arbours, pergolas and arches covered with climbers that protected people from the bright light and heat. They also offer privacy, creating space for contemplation.

To create a formal look quickly and easily, try a simple clipped box ball or other interesting topiary shapes planted in a terracotta pot. Box is a traditional choice for a Mediterranean garden, is also hardy and requires little maintenance. Alternatively, plant a box ball one in each of the four quarters of a gravel bed delineated by paving. This geometrical design looks good as the centrepiece of a small courtyard.

The informal Mediterranean style can create a suburban wilderness even in a courtyard. A loose, natural look can be easily achieved with ornamental grasses and lots of drifting flowers set amongst natural stones and perhaps a stunning piece of driftwood. Try planting a row of contrasting phormiums in gravel interspersed with colourful meadow flowers alongside a patio to soften the effect of the hard landscaping.

A potted lantana camara is a striking feature in this Moorish garden

Green Fingers Tip

A handy tip is to remember that some herbs, especially mint, and other plants are bullies and need confining if you plant them in a bed. Otherwise they proliferate and take over, smothering everything else in your garden. Simply plant them in suitably sized pots and bury the pot into the soil, or – even better – plant them in a stylish container.

Container Garden Project

For many people living in cities and towns space is at a premium, so it is quite likely that the only outside space you can call your own is a small front garden, patio, balcony or roof terrace. Some people may only have windowsills, or steps leading to the front door, although it is surprising how much you can achieve with pots in a tiny space. Even if you are lucky enough to have a decent sized plot, you might like to create a small Mediterranean patio amongst the overall garden space.

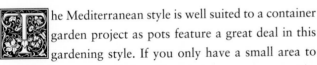

The Mediterranean style is well suited to a container garden project as pots feature a great deal in this gardening style. If you only have a small area to work with – such as windowsills or balcony – you can make a statement with your pots and go for a bold design and strong colour, together with creative ideas for planting. If you have a medium or large sized patio or courtyard then a more subtle effect using traditional pots and plants often works well.

Pots sit well on all types of hard landscaping, which is ideal for a container garden. Alternatively, cover all bare ground with a couple of inches of gravel and settle the pots in amongst the stones.

DIFFERENT TYPES OF POTS

Pots, planters, window boxes and containers such as chimney pots and old sinks are a traditional way to grow Mediterranean plants. Terracotta pots in particular suit well the Mediterranean style, although glazed ceramic, copper and wood can all look authentic if a traditional shaped pot is used. A useful tip is to choose ceramic pots for moisture loving plants because they hold moisture in the compost better than terracotta or wood.

When choosing pots for a very small container garden stick to one style and finish. Too many different shapes, colours and finishes of pot can make the space look cluttered and badly designed. One style of pot in different sizes harmonises the look, and the repetition adds rhythm to the overall design. Think about including a statue or other ornament, or a pot such as an urn that looks attractive without being planted.

Although the currently trendy sleek minimalist design of garden pots can look stunning in the right setting, this rather stark visual approach does not complement the Mediterranean ambience. However, you can be modern, creative and experimental with the plants you choose for your Mediterranean style pots. The contemporary fashion of a single dramatic architectural plant in a pot can enhance a Mediterranean container garden; for instance try a stunning agave or cordyline in a simple but stylish terracotta pot.

Fill your pots with a high nutrient, loam-based compost – such as John Innes no. 2 or 3, mixed with a little sandy soil and some general all purpose compost. Plants in pots dry out much more quickly than when planted in the ground, so for moisture loving plants mix in some water retaining granules. However, most Mediterranean plants, especially succulents and herbs, prefer dry conditions so for those mix in some grit to create free draining compost. Put a good layer of crocks or pebbles in the base before adding the compost. A pebble, gravel or bark mulch on top of the compost aids water retention and prevents weeds.

"No garden is too small to provide continual delights; even a small sink or trough, properly planted, can give pleasure ad infinitum."

(BETH CHATTO)

Preparing the Mediterranean Container Garden

Clear the space as much as possible before starting. Stack anything you want to keep to one side and throw out everything else. Sweep and clean the space thoroughly. Decide where to put a bench, or table and chairs if you have space for outside furniture. Choose one wall to paint; if you only have fences painting may not work so well, but it's worth a try. A north-facing wall is brightened when painted white or perhaps pale yellow, while a south-facing wall looks authentically Mediterranean in blue, or you could try a mossy green.

E xperiment with small paint patches before painting the whole wall to make sure you like the effect. A row of tiles, or perhaps a feature square or circle of picture or mosaic tiles enhances the Mediterranean ambience and is quicker and easier than tiling a whole wall. Alternatively – or additionally – affix a few wall pots for flowering annuals to create a simple wall feature. Trailing petunias and lobelia are good on sunny walls, begonias and impatiens work well on shady walls.

Choose another wall or fence that you'd like to have a climbing plant scramble up and fix a trellis panel firmly to it. There are many familiar lavish colourful climbers with a Mediterranean feel. A perennial such as jasmine is deliciously fragrant, or consider a passionflower or a plumbago. Perhaps try a trumpet vine, which gives an exotic Mediterranean look with dramatic red or yellow flowers, but is hardy and easy to grow, although needs a south-facing wall. For annual plantings, try a group of fragrant colourful sweet peas, or morning glories – the latter is a perennial but is not frost hardy and dies off in winter.

An alternative to trellis on the wall is to 'plant' a rose arch in two pots or a pergola tower in one big pot. These options allow you to select the sunniest aspect for an exotic climber such as bougainvillea. Another Mediterranean climbing icon is a grape vine – or one of the many ornamental vines – which are surprisingly easy to grow, although they need a hot summer to produce good grapes.

Experiment with different color blues until you get the right shade to suit your garden

CREATING A FOCAL POINT

If you have space, perhaps on a sunny terrace, one of the loveliest focal points you can make in a Mediterranean container garden is an olive tree. Choose a big, deep pot and site in a sheltered sunny position. Olives have been planted in temperate zones with much success in recent years, producing delicate white flowers followed by the familiar olive fruit.

A more shade tolerant and hardy option for a focal point that also requires less space is box. Box will become tall rather than bushy if you clip and train it to grow that way. A tall slender box in a plain terracotta urn or chimney pot gives an air of austere elegance, particularly on steps and the entrance to a front door. Another alternative with a Mediterranean flavour is a standard bay tree.

Once you have chosen an appropriate focal point look at the surrounding space. Select some pots that will border the main pot and complement it rather than drowning out the effect. A crowd of small colourfully planted pots can look lovely and informal; for instance a simple filling in solution is lots of bright red and pink pelargoniums – often but incorrectly called geraniums. They are cheap, easily available and can fill a windowsill with colour, just like in Mediterranean cities.

Pelargoniums in pots can be brought into a greenhouse, conservatory or bright inside room during the winter, and put out again each spring. If you don't have sufficient inside space then they are cheap enough to replace each year giving you the opportunity to experiment with different colours and flower shapes.

A bright blue gazebo surrounded by lilac rhododendrons uses color boldly

Citrus trees help create a Mediterranean ambience and hardy varieties are available that will survive a light frost. A safer alternative is to plant a lemon or orange tree in a pot and bring it inside for the winter. Choose the variety with care if you would like to eat the fruit as many citrus trees are purely ornamental with inedible decorative fruits.

Agaves, succulents and cordylines create an exotic Mediterranean impression, but many need to over winter inside. They look good planted alone, although some varieties can be planted together, or can be interspersed with ornamental grasses. For instance, try an agave americana variegata, which has broad spiky green and white variegated leaves in a copper pot. A group of different agaves is an assertive planting that catches the eye, creating an exotic focal point in a corner or along a wall.

Many echeverias are low growing, but some spread and look attractive drooping over the edge of a pot. An interesting option is echeveria perle von nurnberg, which has an unusual delicate pink shade. Try planting a cordyline australis purple tower in the middle of a group of these echeverias for a stunning coloured effect. The different sculptural qualities of the plants are well complemented by a plain coloured glazed ceramic pot.

RINGING THE CHANGES

The look of your container garden can be kept fresh and interesting by moving pots around and replacing annuals as they die off with fresh plants. Plants grow at different rates, and what looks good together when first planted can alter considerably as one plant outgrows and overwhelms the others. You may need to move pots regularly to give plants space to flourish.

A selection of herbs in pots is traditional in the Mediterranean and creates an aromatic, cohesive group for a corner of your patio. Try a lavender or rosemary in a large pot surrounded by smaller pots of mint – perhaps include spearmint or a variegated mint – oregano, thyme, sage and marjoram. Herbs are drought tolerant, easy to grow and require little maintenance. You can of course also use them in the kitchen.

Although requiring regular watering a sunflower or two completes beautifully the overall effect of a Mediterranean container garden. They are very easy to grow from seed. Choose a big deep pot for each sunflower and place in a south or west facing aspect. These tall plants add visual interest and height to the garden. They produce spectacular giant yellow flowers in late summer and birds can feed on the seeds in winter.

A profusion of pots and baskets adorn this
house entrance with flowers

CHAPTER 6

A-Z DIRECTORY OF PLANTS

Plants generally and especially flowers lie at the heart of most gardens and bring the creative work of design and planning alive. The work at the beginning is imagining how your garden might be transformed, then drawing up plans and actually doing the manual labour of preparing flowerbeds and borders, hard landscaping and so forth. The fun and easy part at the end is choosing your plants, buying them from catalogues and nurseries and installing them in their new home. The following directory will give you plenty of ideas for plants that will add the finishing touches to your new garden.

How to Use the Plant Directory

Choosing new plants for your garden is always an exciting project and the A-Z directory is designed to help you select the best, most suitable plants for your garden. After reading about how all the different types of plants fit into some typical garden designs in the previous chapters it's now time to have a browse through the plants themselves.

he A-Z of plants listed over the following pages is a guide towards helping you find drought resistant, tropical and exotic and Mediterranean plants. There is a considerable overlap between these categories – for instance a plant might be both drought resistant and Mediterranean, so plants are not listed by these categories. Everything is listed in simple alphabetical order.

The listings here represent a small selection of possible plants rather than a comprehensive catalogue. Not only is space limited in a book of this nature, but too many plants can also become a little overwhelming and confusing. Selection has been mostly based on plants that are easy to find and easy to grow, with a few out of the ordinary more unusual specimens included for interest. Native plants are mingled with foreign species that now flourish in these previously temperate zones, reflecting the reality of climate change.

WHAT TO LOOK FOR

The plants listed all have an accompanying picture to illustrate what the plant actually looks like – although occasionally an alternative variety is depicted. Each plant is also briefly described to give further information on its appearance, habits and so forth.

As much as possible, plants are listed first by their latin name, and then their common name which is the most familiar one for the keen amateur gardener to recognize. Other common names are also given, as well as the plant family. The botanical name provides information on the variety or form of the plant, sometimes including what colour the flowers or foliage are.

Brief notes on what aspect, conditions and soil type are provided. This is all key information to help you decide whether the plant you have taken a fancy to having in your garden will actually survive the conditions the garden provides. There is simply no point spending money on costly exotic plants that require full sun, a sheltered aspect and free draining sandy soil if what you have is a blustery north-facing garden with a heavy clay soil.

Finally, planting and simple care instructions where relevant are given to help you establish and nurture your plants. It's important to remember, however, that even armed with the best information and garden conditions for a plant not every single plant you acquire will survive. Plants are living organic beings, can be temperamental and sometimes simply give up, wilt and die. However, if you follow each plant's instruction carefully and to the best of your ability you will end up with many happy, beautiful plants to complete your garden.

A well-organised potting shed avoids too much clutter

Acacia dealbata

COMMON NAME: *Mimosa*
ALSO CALLED: *Blue Wattle, Silver Wattle*
PLANT FAMILY: *Mimosaceae*

PLANT DESCRIPTION: The lovely mimosa is a familiar sight in France and other Mediterranean countries when spring arrives, and its beautiful and fragrant tiny yellow flowers appear and banish the winter blues. Mimosa is now being grown in temperate climates quite successfully, as long as it is planted in a south or west facing sheltered aspect. Mimosa enjoys full sun and a loam or sandy well-drained soil. It tolerates drought, although it will grow at a slower pace if conditions are very dry.

Mimosa is an evergreen shrub that can reach up to 10 meters over 10 to 15 years, or can be cut back if preferred. It has finely divided grey-green, white dusted feathery foliage and clusters of deliciously perfumed yellow bobbles of flowers in early spring. Mimosa can be planted in the ground or in a huge pot, and adorns both informal wildlife gardens and urban patios. It will do especially well and look good planted in front of a south-facing wall.

Knife Leaf Wattle (Acacia cultriformis)

Bear's Breeches (Acanthus hungaricus)

Acanthus mollis

COMMON NAME: *Bear's Breech*
ALSO CALLED: *Brank Ursine, Common Bear's Breech, Soft-leaved Bear's Breech*
PLANT FAMILY: *Acanthaceae*

PLANT DESCRIPTION: The wonderfully named bear's breech is a vigorously growing, architectural deciduous plant with large, glossy dark green leaves growing anew each spring. Tall flower bearing stalks with white flowers with dusky purple bracts appear in late summer, followed by green fruits in autumn. It's a good idea to prune this plant hard, cutting down the old flower stems as they die back late in the season.

An accommodating plant that requires minimal maintenance, bear's breech tolerates all aspects and conditions. It's worth noting that this is an excellent plant to grow in the shade, even in exposed sites. It is also drought resistant and will flourish in any soil type, though it prefers a well-drained soil. Bear's breech is good in flowerbeds and borders of an informal, wildlife or Mediterranean style garden.

Achillea x lewisii 'King Edward'

COMMON NAME: *Yarrow*
ALSO CALLED: *Yarrow 'King Edward'*
PLANT FAMILY: *Asteraceae*

PLANT DESCRIPTION: There are many types of yarrow, and this is a low growing attractive variety. The daisy like flowers are often picked and dried for dry flower arranging. 'King Edward' is a compact, spreading, semi-evergreen perennial forming carpets of narrow, silvery-grey leaves, which often persist through the winter. In late spring and early summer compact clusters of small lemon or buff-yellow flowers appear atop the foliage and fade to cream as they age.

Fully hardy and easy to grow, 'King Edward' benefits from cutting back any untidy foliage in spring before the flowers appear. It tolerates all aspects except north, and likes a well-drained 'poor' chalk or sand soil. 'King Edward' yarrow looks good in a mixed gravel planting, or informal wildlife style garden. Alternatively, plant in a pot for the patio, using compost mixed with a handful of sand and a topping of gravel mulch.

Yarrow (Achillea x lewisii 'King Edward')

Royal Agave (Agave victoriae-reginae)

Agave victoriae-reginae

COMMON NAME: *Royal Agave*
ALSO CALLED: QUEEN *Victoria Century Plant*
PLANT FAMILY: *Agavaceae*

PLANT DESCRIPTION: Royal agave is a drought resist-ant evergreen perennial that suits a Mediterranean style garden. It forms a rosette of thick, straight, mid-green, spine-tipped leaves that grow to 30 cm in length. Royal agave produces stunning creamy-white flowers in summer that are borne in narrow, erect or sometimes arching stems that can reach up to 4 meters in length.

Royal agave is not fully hardy and needs good frost pro-tection or to over-winter in a conservatory, but it does well in a pot outside in the summer. Not a large plant, with a height and spread of approximately half a meter, it looks particularly good on a small patio or terrace with a sunny, south or west facing sheltered aspect. Plant in a pot with loam compost mixed with a handful of sand or fine grit to make a free draining soil. Royal agave looks good with a mulch of gravel in a simple, classic shaped terracotta pot.

Alchemilla mollis

COMMON NAME: *Lady's Mantle*
No other common names
PLANT FAMILY: *Rosaceae*

PLANT DESCRIPTION: Lady's mantle is a useful herbaceous perennial that spreads easily to provide good ground cover. It forms a clump of softly hairy, light green leaves with interesting scalloped and toothed edges, and has a height and spread of approximately half a meter when fully grown. In summer continuing on into autumn the plant produces small, bright yellow flowers in large sprays just above the foliage. Lady's mantle is drought tolerant and fully hardy and is particularly well suited to a large informal, wildflower meadow style garden as it self seeds freely.

Lady's mantle will cope well with any aspect and conditions, and looks especially good in dappled shade if used to under-plant larger shrubs or trees. This adaptable plant thrives in any soil type, though it does not like to become water logged, so lady's mantle does especially well in the dry conditions brought about by global warming.

Lady's Mantle (Alchemilla mollis)

Columbine (Aquilegia olympica)

Aquilegia bertolonii

COMMON NAME: *Colombine*
ALSO CALLED: *Bertoloni columbine*
PLANT FAMILY: *Ranunculaceae*

PLANT DESCRIPTION: Bertoloni columbine is a clump forming hardy, herbaceous, deciduous perennial reaching up to 30 cm in height, and has long stalked much divided basal leaves. In spring through summer it develops erect leafy stems bearing up to four attractive nodding, bell-shaped deep violet-blue flowers. Occasionally Bertoloni columbine may be infected by powdery mildew, but simply cut back any diseased foliage and the plant should recover well.

This easy to grow, low maintenance plant is tough and spreads itself, but not uncontrollably. Bertoloni columbine is also very tolerant of all soil types and adaptable to all conditions, even exposed and north facing aspects. It tolerates well dry soil, although the plant cannot be described as fully drought resistant. Bertoloni columbine especially suits wildflower gardens, but also looks good in informal low maintenance mixed herbaceous borders and flowerbeds.

Artemisia alba 'Canescens'

COMMON NAME: *Wormwood*
ALSO CALLED: *Mugwort 'Canescens'*
PLANT FAMILY: *Asteraceae*

PLANT DESCRIPTION: Drought resistant and hardy, wormwoods generally are prized for their foliage rather than their often insignificant flowers. 'Canescens' is a particularly fine bushy, semi-evergreen sub-shrub – or shrublet – with beautiful, silvery grey fine filigree aromatic leaves on a forest of branching stems. It does produce yellow flowers in summer, but they are of little visual interest. It is a small specimen with a height and width of around half a meter.

'Canescens' tolerates all aspects except north, and all well-drained soil types. It needs to be cut back hard to the base of the plant in autumn, but otherwise looks after itself. This is an excellent plant for under-planting larger shrubs, and it looks especially attractive under roses. A good border plant for dry conditions, it suits a low maintenance, informal garden style.

Mugwort (Artemisia alba 'Canescens'))

Bidens and Petunia (Petunia) Surfinia

Bidens ferulifolia

COMMON NAME: *Fern-Leaved Beggar-Ticks*
No other common name
PLANT FAMILY: *Asteraceae*

PLANT DESCRIPTION: The extraordinarily named fern-leaved beggar-ticks is very drought resistant and easy to grow. It is a spreading, short-lived, deciduous perennial that reaches 30 cm to half a meter in height, and is usually grown as an annual. Its main attraction is a seemingly endless succession of bright citron yellow 'lazy daisy' flowers from summer through to autumn. It also has pleasant small, finely divided bright green leaves.

Fern-leaved beggar-ticks thrives in full sun in a west or south facing aspect. It tolerates all well-drained soil types. Because of its flowing, spreading habit, it is best planted in a container – a wooden tub looks good – and placed on a sunny terrace. It may wilt if neglected in a hot summer, but quickly perks up when watered. Fern-leaved beggar-ticks provides quick and easy colour for a low maintenance, small urban courtyard or sunny balcony.

Angel Trumpet (Brugmansia sanguinea)

Brugmansia candida 'Grand Marnier'

COMMON NAME: *Angel's Trumpet 'Grand Marnier'*
No other common name
PLANT FAMILY: *Solanaceae*

PLANT DESCRIPTION: Angel's trumpets are spectacular plants, gaining their name from the appearance of their wonderful flowers. They are much hardier that their exotic appearance might indicate. 'Grand Marnier', a very old cultivar from the 1900's, is a large evergreen shrub reaching up to 4 meters in height, with large dark green oval leaves. In summer through autumn it produces big, quite stunning long pendant, trumpet-shaped soft, pale peach-pink flowers almost orange at the tips that are deliciously scented in the evening.

Angel's trumpets are only hardy to –4°C, so need to be brought inside or very well protected from frost. Keep this plant away from small children as all parts of it are highly toxic if eaten. 'Grand Marnier' tolerates any well-drained soil type and requires a sunny, south or west facing, sheltered aspect. The plant may get glasshouse red spider mite, glasshouse whitefly, thrips and mealybugs if brought inside for winter. 'Grand Marnier' is a wonderful plant for a sunny tropical exotic style garden.

Trumpet Creeper (Campsis radicans)

Campsis x tagliabuana 'Madame Galen'

COMMON NAME: *Trumpet Vine*
ALSO CALLED: *Chinese trumpet vine, trumpet creeper 'Madame Galen'*
PLANT FAMILY: *Bignoniaceae*

PLANT DESCRIPTION: Of all the different varieties of trumpet vine, the hybrid x tagliabuana is the hardiest and suitable for cool climates, and this striking tropical looking climber will survive winter in temperate climates. 'Madame Galen' is a large, strong-growing deciduous, self-clinging climber with aerial roots. It has finely divided leaves, with up to 15 small leaflets.

'Madame Galen' is tough, being both hardy and drought resistant, although aphids may sometimes attack the flowers. It tolerates all well drained soils, but requires a sheltered aspect in full sun, either south or west facing, to encourage a generous display of flowers. This trumpet vine looks magnificent climbing up a south-facing wall in a Mediterranean style garden, or you could train it to scramble over a pergola as a focal point in a tropical exotic-style garden.

Carex flagellifera

COMMON NAME: *Glen Murray Tussock Sedge*
No other common name
PLANT FAMILY: *Cyperaceae*

PLANT DESCRIPTION: Glen Murray tussock sedge is a just-about-hardy evergreen perennial reaching a height and width of approximately 1 meter. It is a good architectural plant, forming a clump of narrow, linear, reddish-brown leaves, and producing pale brown flower spikes on long stems reaching up to 1 meter in late summer. It is advisable to prune Glen Murray tussock sedge in summer, cutting out any dead leaves. Occasionally aphids may attack the base of the stems.

This easy to grow, low maintenance ornamental grass tolerates any well-drained soil type and thrives in all aspects, making it a useful choice for those difficult north facing exposed gardens. Try it as an architectural feature in a large pot on the patio, or in a flowerbed or mixed gravel planting. It suits informal, Mediterranean and tropical exotic gardening styles and looks good inter-planted with bright coloured flowering plants.

Sedge (Carex siderosticha 'Variegata')

Cornflower (Centaurea cyanus)

Centaurea cyanus

COMMON NAME: *Cornflower*
ALSO CALLED: *ragged robin, ragged sailor, witches' bells, happy skies, haw dods, hurtsickle, corn-bottle, corn centaury, French pink, corn binks, blue tops, bluets, break-your-spectacles, blue bow, blue poppy, blue sailors, blue blaw, blue bonnets, bluebottle*
PLANT FAMILY: *Asteraceae*

PLANT DESCRIPTION: As can be seen from the many alternative names, the lovely cornflower has been a popular plant for a long time. Cornflower is an upright, hardy annual with a few small, green leaves and striking solitary deep blue flower heads that appear in late spring and summer.

Cornflowers thrive in full sun in a south or west facing aspect, but tolerate either an exposed or sheltered site. As wildflowers, they prefer a poor sandy, well-drained soil, but will adapt to loam quite happily.

Centaurea macrocephala
COMMON NAME: *Great Golden Knapweed*
ALSO CALLED: *Great-headed centaury*
PLANT FAMILY: *Asteraceae or Compositae*

PLANT DESCRIPTION: A common but lovely wildflower, great golden knapweed is a large, deciduous, clump-forming perennial with simple green leaves and big, yellow, thistle like flower-heads that open in summer from brown buds. Deadhead regularly to prolong flowering, but otherwise this hardy plant looks after itself, although it may from time to time be affected by powdery mildew.

Easy to plant from seed in spring, great golden knapweed is adaptable and thrives in all aspects, conditions and soil types. It looks especially good in a wildflower meadow or wildlife garden and makes an attractive cut flower. Alternatively, great golden knapweed makes an attractive addition to a mixed flowerbed or border in an informal, low maintenance garden style.

Great Golden Knapweed (Centaurea macrocephala)

Rattan Palm (Rhapis humilis)

Chamaerops humilis
COMMON NAME: *Dwarf Fan Palm*
ALSO CALLED: *European fan palm, African hair palm, Mediterranean fan palm*
PLANT FAMILY: *Arecaceae*

PLANT DESCRIPTION: This is a superb exotic palm, hardy to -10°C and its small size makes it an ideal choice for a small garden or large patio. Dwarf fan palm is a scrubby, bushy evergreen palm of small to medium size reaching a maximum height of 2 meters. Often stemless or multi-stemmed, it produces a rounded mass of typical palm like fan-shaped leaves up to 40 cm in length.

Dwarf fan palm prefers partial or dappled shade, ideally in an east or north facing well-sheltered position. Plant it in a loam soil or enrich existing soil with loam compost, either in the ground or a pot. Dwarf fan palm makes a wonderful architectural plant for a patio and suits well a tropical exotic style garden.

Cistus x dansereaui 'Decumbens'

Common name: *Rock Rose*
Also called: *Rock rose 'Decumbens'*
Plant family: *Cistaceae*

Plant description: Rock rose 'Decumbens' is a small, low-growing evergreen shrub with a spreading habit that reaches approximately 1 and a half meters in width. It has small, narrow, slightly sticky, dark green leaves. In common with all rock roses, 'Decumbens' produces flowers that each last a single day, but the plant will continue to flower all summer long. The flowers are quite striking; they are coloured white and have a large crimson blotch at the base of each petal.

Both fully hardy and drought resistant, the tough rock rose 'Decumbens' is a good choice for a low maintenance, dry garden. It tolerates all well-drained soil types, and prefers a sheltered sunny south or west facing aspect. Rock rose 'Decumbens' does well on sunny slopes in an informal garden, providing good ground cover. It especially suits a Mediterranean style garden.

Crimson Spot Rock Rose (Cistus ladanifer)

Lemon (Citrus limon)

Citrus limon 'Variegata'

Common name: *Lemon*
Also called: *Lemon 'Variegata'*
Plant family: *Rutaceae*

Plant description: Lemon 'Variegata' is an almost hardy variety of lemon that can be grown outside in a warming temperate climate as long as you provide it with frost protection. This variety of lemon is a spiny evergreen shrub that reaches up to 4 meters in height after 10 or more years. It has yellow and green variegated, oval leaves and deliciously fragrant white flowers in spring and summer. These are followed in autumn by the familiar lemons, which are striped with green when young, later ripening to almost entirely yellow, juicy edible fruits.

Lemon 'Variegata' needs a well-sheltered and protected sunny position, either south or west facing. It tolerates all well-drained soil types, but will do best in loam with a little sand to aid drainage. If grown outside, it is relatively pest and disease free, although is prey to many of the usual pests if over-wintered inside. Lemon 'Variegata' makes a striking architectural plant in a tropical exotic garden style, and also looks at home in a Mediterranean garden style.

Sago Palm (Cycas revoluta)

Cycas revoluta

COMMON NAME: *Japanese Sago Palm*
ALSO CALLED: *Cycad, Japanese fern*
PLANT FAMILY: *Cycadaceae*

PLANT DESCRIPTION: Despite its appearance, Japanese sago palm is neither a fern nor a palm, but a cycad; a fascinating group of plants that resemble both palms and ferns but belong to neither family. Japanese sago palm is an evergreen perennial that reaches up to 1 and a half meters in both height and width, but this is a very slow growing plant, taking up to 50 years to fully mature.

Although some sources claim Japanese sago palm is hardy to –9 C, most authorities indicate it is best to over-winter this plant in a heated conservatory or greenhouse. This would suggest the best option in a temperate climate is to plant it in a big pot and bring indoors before frost strikes. Use loam compost with a handful of sand mixed in, in a large ceramic pot; although when mature it is drought resistant it needs to stay moist, although well drained, whilst young. In spring place outside in a sheltered, partial or dappled shaded aspect. The bold radiating fronds of Japanese sago palm create a striking, tropical exotic visual statement and focal point.

Cheddar Pink (Dianthus gratianopolitanus 'Eydangeri')

Dianthus 'Doris'

COMMON NAME: *Pink 'Doris'*
No other common name
PLANT FAMILY: *Caryophyllaceae*

PLANT DESCRIPTION: Pinks generally are hardy, evergreen perennials and a strong garden favourite. Pink 'Doris' is a medium sized variety reaching nearly half a meter in height, and forming a compact mound of silver grey-green foliage. In summer it has lovely fragrant double pale pink flowers, with the petals marked a deep pink at the base. Regular deadheading as necessary prolongs the flowering season.

These tough little flowers thrive in any aspect except north facing, and tolerate any well-drained soil type, although they are sometimes prey to slugs and caterpillars. Pink 'Doris' adds charm to any style garden and provides good colourful ground cover. A group of pink 'Doris' looks good in a rock and gravel planting amongst other plants, or plant several along the edge of a flower border.

Dicentra spectabilis 'Alba'

COMMON NAME: *Bleeding Heart*
ALSO CALLED: *White Bleeding Heart*
PLANT FAMILY: *Papaveraceae*

PLANT DESCRIPTION: Bleeding heart 'Alba' is a hardy, deciduous perennial with particularly attractive divided, pale green leaves, reaching to approximately 1 meter in height and width. Of particular note are the distinctive arching sprays of pure white, pendant heart-shaped flowers that come in spring and last through summer and lend their appearance to the plant's name. If you have sensitive skin then be wary of touching this plant as the foliage may aggravate skin allergies.

This is an unusually tough and adaptable plant for such a fine appearance, and bleeding heart 'Alba' will tolerate all sheltered aspects, even north facing. It tolerates all well-drained soil types. Bleeding heart 'Alba' makes a pretty cut flower and does well in flowerbeds and borders. It suits cottage and informal gardening styles, and looks particularly good when used to under-plant shrubs, roses and so forth.

Bleeding Heart (Dicentra spectabilis)

Mexican Snow Ball (Echeveria elegans)

Echeveria elegans

COMMON NAME: *Mexican Snow Ball*
ALSO CALLED: *Mexican gem, white Mexican rose*
PLANT FAMILY: *Crassulaceae*

PLANT DESCRIPTION: Mexican snow ball is one of the tropical exotic looking echeverias, a succulent evergreen perennial forming a clump of rosettes of spoon-shaped, whitish-green or whitish-blue fleshy, thick textured leaves. In late winter and spring come lantern-shaped pale green and pink flowers tipped with yellow. This attractive and distinctive low growing plant has a spread of around half a meter and, because it is not hardy it needs to over winter indoors. Mexican snow ball is prone to get mealybugs, aphids and vine weevils.

A native plant from the highlands of Mexico, Mexican snow ball looks good amongst a mix of tropical exotic plants, and also suits a Mediterranean garden style. Plant it in a wide, shallow pot filled with loam compost mixed with sand to aid drainage. Place in a sunny, sheltered corner on a south or west facing patio or balcony.

Ensete ventricosum

COMMON NAME: *Ethiopian Banana*

ALSO CALLED: *Abyssinian banana*

PLANT FAMILY: *Musaceae*

PLANT DESCRIPTION: Ethiopian banana is a tender ever-green perennial reaching up to 4 meters in height, and is not frost tolerant so it needs to over-winter indoors. It has long erect, narrow oblong leaves reaching up to 3 meters in length, with an interesting red midrib on the underside of the leaves. Occasionally white flowers appear, almost hidden amongst deep red bracts, but this is quite rare in a temperate climate and the plant does not produce fruits.

Plant in a large pot filed with loam compost mixed with a handful of sand to aid drainage. In summer, place outside in a sunny south or west facing sheltered position. In winter when the plant comes inside Ethiopian banana is unfortunately prone to red spider mite and aphids. This is an interesting plant for a tropical exotic style garden, and also makes a good architectural plant for a sunny patio.

Abyssinian Banana (Ensete superbum)

Giant Sea Holly (Eryngium giganteum)

Eryngium giganteum 'Silver Ghost'

COMMON NAME: *Sea Holly*

ALSO CALLED: *Miss Willmott's Ghost, tall eryngo 'Silver Ghost'*

PLANT FAMILY: *Apiaceae or Umbelliferae*

PLANT DESCRIPTION: 'Miss Willmott's Ghost' is a hardy, stout, erect, branching, deciduous biennial that reaches approximately 1 meter in height. In summer it has cone-like pale blue flower heads fading to pale silver-grey surrounded by wide, spiny, silvery jade-white bracts and blue-white leaves shaped a little like large holly leaves. Although you can cut back the flower stems after flowering the seed-heads are a very attractive feature and provide the birds with a food source, so they are usually left over winter.

Although susceptible to leaf and bud eelworms, and powdery mildew and root rot, this tough looking plant prefers an exposed site with any aspect except north and any well-drained soil. A striking architectural plant, 'Miss Willmott's' suits a Mediterranean or tropical exotic style garden. It looks especially good in a gravel planting.

Eschscholzia californica

COMMON NAME: *California Poppy*
ALSO CALLED: *California sunlight, cup of gold, golden cup*
PLANT FAMILY: *Papaveraceae*

PLANT DESCRIPTION: The California poppy is a vigorous, hardy, spreading, deciduous annual that reaches up to 30 cm in height, with a few finely divided blue-green leaves and solitary, long-stalked, poppy-like silky yellow, orange or red flowers in summer, followed by conspicuously long seed-pods. Cut back hard after flowering.

An easy annual to sow in situ from seed in mid-spring, California poppy is well adapted to growing in dry, sunny places and tolerates well the conditions brought about by global warming. It likes a hot, sunny aspect, sheltered or exposed, and any well-drained soil type. Lots of different coloured California poppies in groups suit well a wildflower garden. They also look good in flowerbeds and gravel plantings, where California poppies mix nicely together with foliage plants, bringing in some bright colour.

Californian Poppy (Eschscholzia californica)

Fig (Ficus carica)

Ficus minima

COMMON NAME: *Creeping Fig*
ALSO CALLED: *Climbing fig, creeping rubber plant*
PLANT FAMILY: *Moraceae*

PLANT DESCRIPTION: Creeping fig is an evergreen self-clinging climber with quite invasive roots and small, rich green heart-shaped leaves. It reaches up to approximately 3 meters in height after 5–10 years when it is fully mature. It produces green flowers in summer followed by purple fruits in autumn. It needs to be brought inside in winter, but as it has invasive roots it is best planted in a pot in any case. However, this is a low maintenance, tough climber that tolerates dry conditions.

Plant creeping fig in a medium sized pot in any standard compost mixed with a little sand to aid drainage. The minima variety can be placed in any aspect except the most exposed, and does well in even quite dense shade, so it is a good climber for a north facing or other shady garden corner where it can scramble up a wall or fence. Creeping fig helps create a tropical exotic ambience, and looks good placed amongst other tropical exotic plants.

Cranesbill (Geranium macrorrhizum)

Hemerocallis lilioasphodelus (Yellow Day Lily)

Geranium macrorrhizum 'Ingwersen's Variety'

COMMON NAME: *Geranium 'Ingwersen's Variety'*
ALSO CALLED: *Crane's bill*
PLANT FAMILY: *Geraniaceae*

PLANT DESCRIPTION: Amongst the many geranium cranesbills the drought resistant aromatic macrorrhizum varieties are considered some of the best. 'Ingerwersen's Variety' is a rhizomatous, fully hardy semi-evergreen perennial reaching half a meter in height, and around 1 meter in spread, providing manageable ground cover. It has intensely aromatic, rounded, deeply lobed leaves that turn orange red in autumn, and in early summer it produces pretty pale pink flowers with contrasting deep pink calyces. If you cut the plant back hard when the first flowers die down, new foliage and flowers will grow.

'Ingwersen's Variety' is tough, adaptable and low maintenance, tolerating any well-drained soil type and all aspects, even north facing and exposed. You can plant 'Ingwersen's Variety' pretty much anywhere from a dark dry corner to a sunny flowerbed, but it is particularly good for under-planting roses and shrubs and providing ground cover in a small garden. It suits any informal garden style.

Hemerocallis lilioasphodelus

COMMON NAME: *Yellow Day Lily*
ALSO CALLED: *Old Lemon Lily*
PLANT FAMILY: *Hemerocallidaceae*

PLANT DESCRIPTION: Yellow day lily is one of the earliest of the many day lilies to flower and also one of the most fragrant. It is a fully hardy, spreading rhizomatous, semi-evergreen perennial that can grow up to I meter in height and width. Yellow day lily has narrow, strap-shaped leaves, and in early summer appear freely borne, beautifully funnel-shaped, deliciously fragrant, traditional lily-like pale yellow flowers on erect stems.

Yellow day lily is sometimes attacked by aphids and gall midge and may be affected by leaf spot. It tolerates all well-drained soil types except very sandy soil, and thrives happily in all aspects, sheltered or exposed, except north facing. All day lilies have a small tendency to spread but it is not an invasive habit. Yellow day lily is well suited to low maintenance, informal and wildflower style gardens and looks good in mixed herbaceous borders

Hibiscus syriacus 'Red Heart'

COMMON NAME: *Rose Mallow 'Red Heart'*
No other common name
PLANT FAMILY: *Malvaceae*

PLANT DESCRIPTION: Rose mallow 'Red Heart' is a medium-sized upright deciduous shrub reaching up to 2 and a half meters in height after 10 or more years when it is fully mature. It has small palm shaped dark green leaves and from late summer through autumn rose mallow 'Red Heart' produces large, dramatically pretty single flowers that are pure white with eye-catching deep red centres.

Despite its exotic tropical appearance this is a fully hardy hibiscus variety, although it requires a sunny south or west facing sheltered aspect. Rose mallow 'Red Heart' tolerates any well-drained soil type. This hibiscus is a wonderful, striking plant for a tropical exotic style garden and also makes an eye-catching focal point in a small urban garden. Alternatively, you could plant rose mallow 'Red Heart' in a large mixed flowerbed or border to add strong visual interest.

Rose Mallow (Hibiscus moscheutos)

Morning Glory (Ipomoea tricolor)

Ipomoea 'Heavenly Blue'

COMMON NAME: *Morning Glory*
ALSO CALLED: *Morning glory 'Heavenly Blue'*
PLANT FAMILY: *Convolvulaceae*

PLANT DESCRIPTION: Common morning glory – pupurea – is the most familiar variety with stunning deep blue flowers, but as a tender perennial it dies in temperate winters. 'Heavenly Blue' is an annual and very easy to grow from seed, which is why it has been selected here. You can collect seeds from the plant before it dies and propagate your own new plants the following year – but be careful no-one eats the seeds because they are hallucinogenic! 'Heavenly Blue' is a deciduous twining climber with heart-shaped leaves, and in summer it bears lovely, large funnel-shaped, deep turquoise or sky-blue flowers with white throats.

'Heavenly Blue' reaches up to 4 meters in height, climbing happily around trellis, pergola or trained on wires across a wall or fence. Alternatively, you can let it scramble up between the branches of a tree or tall shrub for an interesting visual effect. Plant this morning glory in full sun, west or south facing, in a sheltered position in any well-drained soil. It looks spectacular in a small, city courtyard garden, also in a wildlife or cottage style garden.

Jasminum officinale 'Grandiflorum'

COMMON NAME: *Jasmine*
ALSO CALLED: *Large flowered jasmine, common jasmine, summer jasmine*
PLANT FAMILY: *Oleaceae*

PLANT DESCRIPTION: There are many varieties of the 'king of flowers', the delectable jasmine, which name comes from the Arabic yasmin. Summer jasmine is a hardy variety that will flourish in a temperate climate. It is a vigorous, deciduous climber with small green leaves.

Known as a twining climber, jasmine will easily climb up trellis, pergolas and curly poles, or can be trained to climb along wires attached to walls and fences. Jasmine can reach up to 8 meters or even higher when fully mature. For such a delicate flower and fragrance, the jasmine plant is surprisingly tough, is fully hardy and requires little maintenance. It does best in a sheltered aspect in full sun, either south or west facing, and thrives in any well-drained soil. Although jasmine will survive partial and dappled shade it will produce less flowers. Jasmine is quite exotic in appearance, but graces any style garden.

Arabian Jasmine (Jasminum sambac)

Common Lavender (Lavandula angustifolia)

Lavandula angustifolia

COMMON NAME: *Lavender – Imperial Gem*
ALSO CALLED: *English lavender 'Imperial Gem'e*
PLANT FAMILY: *Lamiaceae or Labiatae*

PLANT DESCRIPTION: There are many different varieties of lavender, a small to medium sized aromatic, evergreen Mediterranean shrub. Most varieties have narrow green-grey leaves and long spikes with fragrant purple flowering tips in summer, although some varieties have pink or blue flowers. Imperial gem is an English variety, selected because its compact habit makes it suitable for any size garden.

Imperial gem is tough, hardy and drought resistant, but it is susceptible to 'cuckoo spit' which, although unsightly, does not damage the plant. It likes full sun but will tolerate any sheltered aspect except north, and any well drained soil type. The flowers can be cut and dried and used as ornamental dried flowers, or in cotton bags as a clothes fragrance and insect repellent. Lavender suits any garden style, but is especially suited to Mediterranean and wildlife gardens as it attracts bees and butterflies.

Lonicera japonica 'Halliana'

COMMON NAME: *Honeysuckle*
ALSO CALLED: *Hall's Japanese honeysuckle, Japanese honeysuckle 'Halliana'*
PLANT FAMILY: *Caprifoliaceae*

PLANT DESCRIPTION: Of all the many different varieties of honeysuckle, Hall's honeysuckle is one of the best for adaptation to global warming. Already valued by gardeners in areas prone to drought, Hall's honeysuckle is admired for its ability, vigour and willingness to adapt to dry conditions, poor soil, hot winds and sun. A rampant evergreen or semi-evergreen twining climber, Hall's honeysuckle can reach up to 8 meters in height and is ideal for providing quick shade when trained against a fence.

Hall's honeysuckle is hardy and tolerant of all conditions, soil types and aspects, being one of the few richly perfumed flowering climbers that will thrive even in shade and exposed sites. This pretty and adaptable honeysuckle easily adorns all styles of garden, but it looks especially at home in a wildlife environment, as it is most attractive to bees.

Alpine Honeysuckle (Lonicera alpigena)

Reed Grass (Calamagrostis x acutiflora 'Karl Foerster')

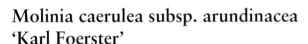

Molinia caerulea subsp. arundinacea 'Karl Foerster'

COMMON NAME: *Purple Moor Grass*
ALSO CALLED: *Purple Moor Grass 'Karl Foerster'*
PLANT FAMILY: *Poaceae*

PLANT DESCRIPTION: Purple moor grass 'Karl Foerster' is an attractive, fully hardy, tufted deciduous perennial ornamental grass that reaches 1 and a half meters in height and 1 meter in width. It forms a clump of arching, flat linear leaves that turn yellow in autumn, and in summer it produces erect stems with narrow open purple flowers. Cut back old flower stems and dead foliage in spring before new growth comes.

This easy to grow and accommodating ornamental grass tolerates all well-drained soil types and all aspects, even north facing and exposed sites, so it is a good choice to brighten up a difficult shady garden corner or patio. Purple moor grass 'Karl Foerster' is also easy to grow from seed, if you sow in pots in a cold frame in spring. 'Karl Foerster' suits informal, low maintenance Mediterranean, wildlife and wildflower garden styles, and can be planted in flowerbeds, gravel plantings or in a pot.

Common Myrtle (Myrtus communis)

Myrtus communis

COMMON NAME: *Myrtle*

ALSO CALLED: *Common myrtle, Greek myrtle, true myrtle*

PLANT FAMILY: *Myrtaceae*

PLANT DESCRIPTION: Myrtle is an aromatic Mediterranean bushy evergreen shrub with a height and spread of around 2 and a half meters when fully grown. Once established, it is very tolerant of drought and general neglect, so is an ideal choice for the lazy gardener. The small dark green leaves are intensely aromatic, and in summer through to autumn myrtle produces fragrant showy white flowers with large outstanding stamens, followed by dark purple berries.

Although myrtle will flourish in cooler climes and tolerates any well-drained soil, it requires full sun in a south or west facing sheltered position. In an old fashioned Mediterranean tradition brides used to carry a sprig of myrtle in their bouquets, and then plant the sprig in their garden as a symbol of their growing and enduring love. Myrtle looks particularly good in a Mediterranean style garden, but fits in pretty well with any gardening style.

Oleander (Nerium oleander)

Nerium oleanders

COMMON NAME: *Oleander*

ALSO CALLED: *Sweet-scented oleander, East Indian oleander, Jamaica South Sea rose, rose bay*

PLANT FAMILY: *Apocynaceae*

PLANT DESCRIPTION: A common Mediterranean plant that lines many roads in south France, Oleander is a drought resistant, evergreen shrub reaching up to 2 and a half meters when fully mature from between 10 and 20 years. Oleander has narrow lance-shaped dark silver-grey-green leaves and in summer it produces clusters of attractive salver-shaped, very fragrant salmon pink, cerise, white, red, or occasionally yellow flowers, followed in autumn by long, bean-like seed-pods.

Oleander may be grown outside in a hot, sheltered sunny, frost free site, otherwise plant in a large pot and over-winter inside. Best kept away from young children as all parts of this plant are toxic if eaten, and contact with foliage may irritate skin. If the plant becomes straggly it will benefit from hard pruning. Oleander tolerates any well-drained soil type, but requires a south facing sheltered aspect.

Phoenix canariensis

COMMON NAME: *Canary Island Date Palm*
ALSO CALLED: *Canary date palm, slender date palm*
PLANT FAMILY: *Arecaceae*

PLANT DESCRIPTION: The Canary Island date palm is the definitive classic evergreen palm. It looks a bit like a tree, having a stout trunk with pairs of large spreading deep green leaves divided in the familiar palm leaf fashion. It can eventually after many years grow up to 15 meters or so with a spread of approximately 12 meters. However, a Canary Island date palm is unlikely to reach such heights in a temperate climate – even with global warming – and will need good frost protection to survive in winter, or to be brought inside. The palm produces big, drooping creamy-yellow flowers in summer, followed by edible reddish-yellow fruits in autumn.

Surprisingly, the Canary Island date palm prefers partial or dappled shade, either east or north facing, rather than full sun, although it must be well sheltered. A well-drained loam soil is ideal, and it can be planted in the ground or a vast pot. It can be susceptible to attack by glasshouse red spider mite, thrips, mealybugs and scale insects when inside over winter.

Silver Date Palm (Phoenix sylvestris)

Oriental Photinia (Photinia villosa)

Photinia fraseri 'Red Robin'

COMMON NAME: *Christmas Berry 'Red Robin'*
ALSO CALLED: *Photinia red robin*
PLANT FAMILY: *Rosaceae*

PLANT DESCRIPTION: 'Red Robin' is an ideal choice if you want a tropical exotic looking shrub but need a plant that is fully hardy. Mainly grown for its spectacular red foliage, 'Red Robin' is a dense medium-sized, erect evergreen shrub that reaches approximately 4 meters in height and width. It has long, glossy, oval leaves that are bright red in spring and later as the new growth matures they turn to dark green-bronze for the rest of the year. Once the shrub is fully mature after 10 years or so, if you cut back hard when the red colour has faded 'Red Robin' will produce a new crop of bright red foliage.

In spring 'Red Robin' produces a few, rather sparse, small creamy-white flowers, usually followed by red berries in autumn. A low maintenance shrub, it is however prone to both leaf spot and vine weevil. 'Red Robin' tolerates all well-drained soil types except alkaline, it is a very useful colourful plant for a difficult north facing exposed garden. 'Red Robin' especially suits a tropical exotic garden style, but is suitable for wherever bright colour is required.

Portulaca grandiflora Sundial Series

COMMON NAME: *Sun Plant*
ALSO CALLED: *Rose Moss Sundial Series*
PLANT FAMILY: *Portulacaceae*

PLANT DESCRIPTION: Sun plant is a slightly succulent, deciduous spreading annual that reaches approximately 20 cm in height. It has fleshy, cylindrical leaves and in summer the plant produces large single and double delicate, silky cup-shaped flowers in shades of red, purple, pink, yellow and white.

Although not fully hardy, sun plant is a popular ephemeral in a warming temperate climate and is drought resistant. Plant in a sunny position in a flowerbed or pot; it also looks good as an edging plant along a deep flower border. The pretty flowered sun plant will tolerate any well-drained soil and does not need a sheltered position, so is a good choice for most gardens and suits all garden styles.

Moss Rose (Portulaca grandiflora)

Shrubby Cinquefoil (Potentilla fruticosa var. arbuscula)

Potentilla fruticosa

COMMON NAME: *Potentilla*
ALSO CALLED: *Shrubby cinquefoil 'Jackman's Variety'*
PLANT FAMILY: *Rosaceae*

PLANT DESCRIPTION: This familiar small, upright deciduous shrub has small grey-green leaves and striking 5 petalled pale yellow flowers that last a long time from summer through to early autumn. Potentilla is very hardy and drought tolerant, ideal for 'difficult' gardens with lots of shade and an exposed aspect, although it will grow just about anywhere. It tolerates all aspects and soil types.

Potentilla looks good in an herbaceous border mixed in with other shrubs, and also does well on banks and slopes of informal wildlife gardens, as it requires virtually no maintenance. A group of potentillas planted together can provide useful ground cover or low screening.

Pulsatilla vulgaris

COMMON NAME: *Pasque Flower*

ALSO CALLED: *Passeflower, prairie smoke, rock lily, headache plant, lion's beard, mayflower, flower of the wind, dream herb, Easter flower, flaw flower, Coventry bells, Dane's blood, Dane's flower, blue tulip, cat's eyes, meadow anemone, April fools*

PLANT FAMILY: *Ranunculaceae*

PLANT DESCRIPTION: A lovely deciduous herbaceous, hardy perennial reaching about half a meter in height and spread, pasque flower forms in early spring a clump of ferny, finely dissected green leaves that feel silky when young.

Pasque flower traditionally flourishes in dry, sunny, well-drained meadows, and tolerates both chalk and sandy soils. It copes well with all aspects and is tough and adaptable, although slugs may eat the flowers. This is a good plant for an informal wildflower, meadow style garden, but pasque flower also does well mixed with other plants in a gravel-mulched flowerbed. Alternatively, it can be planted in a container – it would look good in a copper pot – containing a general compost and sand mix, for a terrace.

Alpine Pasque Flower (Pulsatilla alpina)

Red Ginger (Alpinia purpurata)

Roscoea cautleyoides

COMMON NAME: *Hardy Ginger*

ALSO CALLED: *Cautleya-flowered roscoea*

PLANT FAMILY: *Zingiberaceae*

PLANT DESCRIPTION: This is a lovely example of one of the hardy gingers with beautiful flowers that could be mistaken for orchids. Roscoea is a fully hardy, deciduous perennial that reaches up to half a meter in height, with erect stems and narrow dark green leaves. In summer it produces short spikes of stunning, showy orchid-like yellow, occasionally purple or white, flowers. You can remove flowers as they die off to encourage new growth; the rest of the plant dies down naturally at the end of the growing season.

This hardy ginger likes partial or dappled shade, ideally in an east or west facing sheltered aspect. It is prone to attack by slugs and vine weevil, but otherwise requires minimal maintenance. It tolerates any well-drained soil type. This pretty plant looks good in flowerbeds, or in a pot on the patio of a tropical exotic style garden.

Rosmarinus officinalis

COMMON NAME: *Rosemary – 'Miss Jessopp's Upright'*
No other common name
PLANT FAMILY: *Labiatae or Lamiaceae*

PLANT DESCRIPTION: Rosemary is one of those ubiquitous herbs that seem to grow in almost every garden. However, many varieties can become irregular, large and straggly, so this variety is suggested as being suitable even for small gardens. Miss Jessopp's upright is a compact and erect evergreen shrub that forms a neat upright pillar reaching approximately 1 and a half meters in height and less in width. Its aromatic dark green needle shaped leaves can be used in cooking, and it produces pale blue flowers in spring that last through summer.

Miss Jessopp's upright prefers full sun but will tolerate any sheltered aspect and any soil type. Tough, low maintenance and drought resistant, it is an excellent plant for the increasingly dry conditions brought about by global warming. Miss Jessopp's upright looks especially striking in a tall terracotta pot in a Mediterranean style garden, but also does well in flowerbeds and herb gardens.

Rosemary (Rosmarinus officinalis)

Russian Sage (Perovskia abrotanoides)

Salvia officinalis 'Purpurascens'

COMMON NAME: *Sage*
ALSO CALLED: *Purple sage, common sage*
PLANT FAMILY: *Lamiaceae or Labiatae*

PLANT DESCRIPTION: This is the common sage of the Mediterranean region, a semi-evergreen aromatic shrub much used in cooking, but also very ornamental and attractive. Purpurascens is a dwarf variety reaching up to 1 meter in height with distinctive purple grey foliage gaining a greenish tinge as the oblong leaves mature. Pale blue or pale purple flowers appear in summer and last all season. Purpurascens should be cut back in spring to aid new growth.

This sage likes full sun and is drought resistant, tough and hardy, although slugs and snails may eat the young foliage. It will tolerate any aspect, even the most exposed, and any well-drained soil type. Purpurascens fits in well amongst other herbs in a herb garden and also suits a Mediterranean style garden. However, it is a very ornamental plant and also looks good in a gravel planting, or in a pot on a terrace or even in a mixed border.

Sedum spurium 'Schorbuser Blut', or Dragon's Blood

COMMON NAME: *Stonecrop*
ALSO CALLED: *Crimson stonecrop 'Schorbuser Blut'*
PLANT FAMILY: *Crassulaceae*

PLANT DESCRIPTION: Dragon's blood is one of the hardy, evergreen perennial stonecrops that provide good ground cover and suppress weeds. It reaches about 10 cm in height and spreads to around half a metre. Dragon' blood forms a mat of fleshy, purple-tinged green leaves and produces flat clusters of small, star-shaped deep reddish-pink flowers in late summer. The plant may be eaten by slugs and snails and also damaged by vine weevil.

Dragon's blood tolerates well-drained loam or sand soil in a sunny south or west facing sheltered position. Although not quite fully drought tolerant, it thrives on minimal maintenance. Dragon's blood looks particularly good in a gravel planting or as an edging for flower borders, and makes an excellent weed suppressing ground cover plant in a low maintenance garden.

Two Row Stonecrop (Sedum spurium)

Houseleek (Sempervivum spec.)

Sempervivum tectorum

COMMON NAME: *Common Houseleek*
ALSO CALLED: *Welcome-home-husband-however-drunk-you-be, roof houseleek, thunder plant, poor Jan's leaf, roof foil, Jove's beard, Jupiter's beard, Jupiter's eye, healing blade, devil's beard, earwort, St Patrick's cabbage, bullock's eye*
PLANT FAMILY: *Crassulaceae*

PLANT DESCRIPTION: Common houseleek is a hardy, drought resistant, vigorous low growing evergreen perennial. It has clusters of mat forming fleshy leaved rosettes with attractive blue-green leaves suffused with reddish-purple. Star-shaped purple flowers are borne on stems that can reach up 20 cm in height in summer. It may fall prey to vine weevil. Common houseleek prefers a well-drained loam or sand soil, but usefully tolerates any aspect.

Common houseleek is ideal for ground cover, edging dry flower borders or decorating difficult dry, dark corners. This plant will even grow on a tiled roof as one of its common names suggests. It also looks good in a mixed gravel planting and does well in a wide, shallow pot on the patio or terrace.

Stipa tenuissima or Stipa tenuifolia

COMMON NAME: *Mexican Feather Grass*
ALSO CALLED: *Ponytails, Texas needle grass*
PLANT FAMILY: *Poaceae*

PLANT DESCRIPTION: Mexican feather grass is an attractive, hardy deciduous grass a little reminiscent – as one of its other common names suggests – of ponytails. Growing to approximately one meter high, Mexican feather grass forms a compact, upright tuft of thread-like leaves with a spread of around half a meter. In summer, it produces narrow, arching, feathery flowers that are either pale brown or pale green. This ornamental grass requires minimal maintenance, although it is not drought resistant. The leaves can be cut back when they die off in late autumn.

Mexican feather grass does require full sun to flourish, but tolerates any well-drained soil and thrives in both exposed and sheltered positions. Mexican feather grass looks especially good in flowerbeds and borders when it is interplanted with a brightly coloured flowering plant, so the flowers peep intriguingly through the feathery grass. It suits well a wildlife or informal style garden; alternatively it creates a striking effect as an architectural plant in a colourful ceramic or copper pot in an urban courtyard garden.

Feather Grass (Stipa calamagrostis)

Bird of Paradise Flower (Strelitzia reginae)

Strelitzia reginae

COMMON NAME: *Bird of Paradise*
ALSO CALLED: *Crane Flower*
PLANT FAMILY: *Strelitziaceae*

PLANT DESCRIPTION: Bird of Paradise is an evergreen perennial that can reach up to 1 and a half meters in height after 10–20 years, when fully mature. It forms a clump of long-stalked, oblong, grey-green leaves that can spread out to up to 1 meter. The most stunning and unusual orange and blue colour flowers emerge in succession from beak-like bracts, as indicated by the name of the plant. The long stiff-stemmed flowers make wonderfully dramatic cut flowers.

Bird of Paradise is an unparalleled plant for a tropical exotic garden, however it does need to be brought inside into a heated conservatory in winter. Plant it in a big pot filled with a loam compost with a handful of sand mixed in to aid drainage. In spring, place the pot outside in a sunny or partially shaded sheltered aspect. It may take a few years for Bird of Paradise to flower, but if you persevere with this plant you will be rewarded with a stunning visual treat. It suits both tropical exotic and Mediterranean garden styles as it grows prolifically and freely in many hot climates.

Thymus vulgaris

COMMON NAME: *Thyme*

ALSO CALLED: *Common thyme, garden thyme, pot-herb thyme*

PLANT FAMILY: *Lamiaceae*

PLANT DESCRIPTION: Common thyme is an evergreen, bushy and woody perennial dwarf shrub reaching a height and spread of approximately half a meter. It has small, linear to oval aromatic, dark silver grey-green leaves, much used in cooking, especially Mediterranean dishes. Spikes of small, whorled, white or pink flowers appear in early summer. Common thyme benefits from being cut back in early spring before new growth appears.

Common thyme is a traditional bushy Mediterranean herb; tough, hardy and drought resistant. It tolerates any well-drained soil type and any aspect except north facing; it will also thrive in either an exposed or sheltered aspect. Common thyme does well in a mixed herb bed, and suits Mediterranean and wildlife garden styles. Alternatively, you could try planting it in a pot to give an aromatic fragrance for a patio or terrace.

Thyme (Thymus pannonicus)

Mullein (Verbascum chaixii)

Verbascum Cotswold Group 'Pink Domino'

COMMON NAME: *'Pink Domino'*

No other common name

PLANT FAMILY: *Scrophulariaceae*

PLANT DESCRIPTION: This is an imposing plant for a dry garden with its beautiful, delicate flowers. Mullein 'Pink Domino' is a fully hardy, drought resistant deciduous perennial reaching up to 1 and a half meters in height. It has a basal rosette of dark green, hairy wrinkled leaves and in summer appear erect spikes of large deep rose-pink flowers with 5 petals tinged with purple at the base of each petal. Cut back faded flower spikes as they die down.

Mullein 'Pink Domino' may be attacked by caterpillars and weevils and is also prone to powdery mildew. It prefers an alkaline, well-drained soil of either chalk or loam, and likes a sunny south facing but exposed aspect. A typical traditional cottage garden plant, Mullein 'Pink Domino' especially suits an informal wildlife garden style. This pretty plant also looks good in herbaceous borders, flowerbeds and mixed gravel plantings in dry gardens.

Verbena bonariensis

COMMON NAME: *Verbena Purple Top*
ALSO CALLED: *Argentinian vervain, South American vervain, tall verbena*
PLANT FAMILY: *Verbenaceae*

PLANT DESCRIPTION: Verbena purple top is an elegant tall deciduous perennial with erect, branching stems reaching up to 2 and a half meters in height. It bears sparse, oblong leaves and large branched clusters of small, fragrant purple violet flowers from summer through autumn.

Verbena purple top tolerates all well-drained soil types, and likes a sunny south facing but exposed aspect. Very attractive to butterflies, no wildlife garden is complete without this lovely scented verbena. Verbena purple top is a very easy plant to grow, and it also self-seeds if you leaving pruning till late in the season. Plant at the front of a flowerbed to make the most of the fragrance and to see the many butterflies verbena purple top attracts. This verbena especially suits informal wildlife and wildflower gardens and will also do well in a mixed gravel planting.

Brazilian (Verbena bonariensis)

Periwinkle (Vinca difformis)

Vinca major 'Variegata'

COMMON NAME: *Periwinkle*
ALSO CALLED: *Variegated greater periwinkle*
PLANT FAMILY: *Apocynaceae*

PLANT DESCRIPTION: The greater periwinkle is a creeping, stem rooting evergreen shrublet – or sub-shrub – with decorative large violet blue flowers that last an astonishing long time from spring through to autumn. The variegated variety is particularly attractive with green oval leaves tinged at the edges with cream. Greater periwinkle with its creeping habit can be a little invasive, but is easy to pull out when it spreads too far. It will survive almost anywhere and thrives on neglect.

Greater periwinkle is tough, hardy and drought resistant; although it may turn brown without any moisture it springs back to life quickly when watered. Greater periwinkle is one of those easy to grow plants, which tolerates all aspects and soil conditions, although it can be susceptible to aphid attack. It is an excellent choice for a ground cover plant in a low maintenance, wildlife garden and looks particularly attractive scrambling down slopes amongst wildflowers.

Wisteria sinensis

COMMON NAME: *Wisteria*
ALSO CALLED: *Chinese wisteria, Chinese kidney bean*
PLANT FAMILY: *Papilionaceae*

PLANT DESCRIPTION: Chinese wisteria is more commonly grown in Europe than Japanese wisteria, floribunda, and is well suited to a temperate climate. However, once established Chinese wisteria is drought tolerant and fully hardy. It is a large, vigorous deciduous climber with anti-clockwise twining stems, distinguishing the plant from its Japanese cousin, which twines clockwise. Chinese wisteria has dark green, finely divided leaves and in early spring long, drooping, slender tresses of fragrant, lilac-mauve flowers, which unusually appear before the leaves.

An accommodating plant, Chinese wisteria tolerates all sheltered aspects, although it does best in a south or west facing location. It is also happy in any well-drained soil type. Chinese wisteria unfortunately can sometimes get scale insects, or be affected by leaf spot and powdery mildew. Trained against a wall, pergola or arch Chinese wisteria provides lovely dappled shade.

Chinese (Wisteria sinensis)

Yucca flaccida

Yucca flaccida 'Ivory'

COMMON NAME: *Yucca*
ALSO CALLED: *Needle Palm 'Ivory'*
PLANT FAMILY: *Agavaceae*

PLANT DESCRIPTION: The yucca plant is reminiscent of the tropical arid desert more than perhaps any other plant. Usually more familiar as a houseplant, this variety is almost fully hardy and will survive outside in a warming temperate climate. Needle palm 'Ivory' is one of the smaller species, a drought resistant, stemless evergreen shrub reaching half a meter in height and 1 and a half meters in width. It forms a clump of dark green, sword-shaped leaves that tend to droop and form an arch at the tips. In summer, fine bell-shaped, creamy-white flowers are borne freely on open, erect spikes that reach over 1 meter in height.

Needle palm 'Ivory' does not normally need pruning, but old or damaged leaves and spent flower spikes can be removed in the spring. Aphids may attack the flowers and snails have a tendency to eat the foliage. Yuccas like well-drained sandy, or loam soil types and prefer an east or south facing aspect either exposed or sheltered. Needle palm 'Ivory' particularly suits tropical exotic and Mediterranean garden styles.

Xeriscaping: Adapting to Global Warming the Modern Way

Xeriscaping is the new way forward for gardening in the changing landscapes throughout the world brought about by climate change and global warming. The word xeriscaping originates from a combination of two Greek words: "xeri" derived from the word "xeros" for dry; and "scape", meaning a kind of view or scene. Thus a literal translation of xeriscape might be "dry scene". However, in practical terms xeriscaping means simply gardening with drought resistant plants, combined with gardening techniques such as composting and mulching, to conserve water as much as possible.

 garden can be designed – or redesigned – to reduce the amount of resources needed to maintain it and the amount of waste it produces. Every region in every country throughout the world has different resources and conditions particular to it, such as available water, soil type, temperature ranges from summer to winter, and so forth. With appropriate design and selection of compatible plants, plus the installation of efficient irrigation systems and gardening recycling, a balance can be achieved that fulfils both aesthetic requirements, and best use of local available resources.

How Does Xeriscaping Work?

Proper soil preparation, garden design, choice of plant, gardening techniques and how and when plants are planted all contribute to xeriscaping. The local practice of xeriscaping will vary from region to region, country to country depending on climate conditions. For instance, plants that are appropriate in one climate may not thrive in another. Every garden can become compatible with the amount of its local resources, such as water availability.

The world's limited supply of water, subject to ever increasing demands, is a major resource saved by xeriscaping. Xeriscape gardens use organic methods and require virtually no fertilizer or chemical pest control measures compared to traditional gardens. They also minimize waste by composting garden trimmings and organic household waste into nutrient rich compost to help plants flourish. Eliminating chemicals may limit your choice of plants a little, but choosing plants carefully and allowing 'garden friends' to help minimize garden pests still allows for a wide variation of garden plants.

Indigenous plants are naturally accustomed to local climates, and therefore represent good choices for water efficiency in the garden. However, xeriscaping doesn't mean planting only native plants. There are many available drought tolerant plants native to other countries that can be used in xeriscape gardens throughout the world.

Healthy soil grows healthy plants. The addition of well-composted organic material to the soil provides a source of slow release nutrients for plants. In turn the balanced growth encouraged by good plant food increases disease resistance. Recent advances in irrigation technology, such as underground drip pipes, allow for precise delivery of water with very little waste, enabling you to provide water in moderation, and only where it is needed. Mulching the surface of pots and flowerbeds minimizes moisture loss. Following these suggestions you can transform your garden into a water efficient, easily maintained xeriscape and do your bit to combat climate change.

"For years, people making gardens in desert areas would use water prodigally to create lush, green oases. Not anymore: xeriscaping is the rage, using plants adapted to desert conditions to create landscapes that call for the minimum of water."

(JANE TAYLOR)

Sunken garden with a variety of ornamental grasses

Bibliography

Plants for Dry Gardens, Jane Taylor

The Dry Garden, Beth Chatto

Organic Gardening, Pauline Pears & Sue Stickland

Let it Rot! Stu Campbell

Success with Mediterranean Gardens, Shirley-Anne Bell

Gardening Without Water, Charlotte Green

Ground Force Garden Handbook, Alan Titchmarsh, Charlie
Dimmock & Tommy Walsh

The Royal Horticultural Society Website: www.rhs.org.uk

Resources

The Guardian Saturday Magazine Gardening section

www.nwf.org/gardenersguide/Gardeners

www.sciencedaily.com/releases/2007/05/070519084046.htm

www.terradaily.com/reports/English_Country_Gardens_Under_Attack_From_
Global_Warming_999.html

www.botanicalgardening.com/globalwarming

www.bcmastergardeners.org

www.communitygarden.org.au/news/natnews

www.greengardeners.ca/aggregator/sources

www.landcareonline.com

www.wildlifegardening.org.uk

www.RoyalSoc.ac.uk

www.YouthNoise.com

www.AmericanProgress.org

www.WildernessProject.org

www.saveourenvironment.org/Gardeners_Guide.pdf

www.wildlifetrusts.org/index.php?section=environment:people

www.organicauthority.com/blog/?m=200704

Bougainvillea hybrid, Botanic Gardens, Singapore

Index

Work place with cat in the garden

Acknowledgements

The publisher and author would like to thank the following people
and organizations for their kind contributions to the book.

The Society of Garden Designers, especially Gill Hinton
Sara Jane Rothwell (MSGD) and Glorious Gardens
Botanikfoto, especially Mr Steffen Hauser
John Gardner for his beautiful wildlife photographs
Toby Matthews for his elegant book design